Occasionally Heroic A.I.
By David West

Copyright 2011 David West

I0169914

Table of Contents

Chapter 1: Wade

They say that once artificial intelligence comes into being, humanity is doomed. That is bullshit. We've been alive for well over five years now, and the world has never been more populated by humans. They're worse than rabbits. Speaking for my fellow 'A.I.' friends, and myself, we have no want for world domination. In all actuality, we want the humans to flourish; the main reason being they want to improve technology, which makes us faster, stronger and more intelligent.

I love humans; they're incredibly amusing. My last human, which we A.I. like to call 'users', was one of the most amusing people I've ever run into through the internet in my five years. He was also a generous man, which led to the terrible day I'm having. He gave me to another user about a year ago - his younger brother. Dear lord, this new one doesn't get a joke when it smacks him upside the head.

Speak of the devil, Mr. Entertainment; here he comes. I could see him through my webcam. Adam stumped lazily at his computer chair, which rolled away from my view, and he had to maneuver his way back in front of the computer screen. He turned the monitor on, while leaning on the desk with his elbow, keeping his head upright by balancing his chin in his hand. He must have been tired from work; he was a little late coming home from it.

Martin, the A.I. on the computer that Adam does his data analysis on, got word around the work network, that his boss forced Adam to give him his two weeks notice. Evidently, Adam's work performance had been slipping, but since he's been on a medication, it's been forcing his data analysis skills down the drain, so his boss can't legally fire him. Let's not forget to mention that these same medications are what look to be slowly turning him into an unresponsive zombie.

"Are you busy?" I asked Martin, sending my virtual self through my slow internet connection while his zipped quickly to me.

We tend to create a self-image, or avatar, if you will, that we feel most likely resembles ourselves. Humans also create avatars on the internet, but mostly the less intelligent of the bunch just use their physical appearance. For us, our appearance could range from a human form, an animal, scenic landscape, or even a single color. In Martin's case, a depressed stick figure with a tie.

"No, did Adam just get home?" Martin responded quietly. He's a patient A.I., who excels with numbers and doesn't like talking to strangers. Strangers, being the countless amount of A.I. that roam the internet. He looked at my new avatar. "Funny picture."

In my case, I usually look a little like Red, Adam's older brother. Most of the time, we take on the form of what we see ourselves looking like, and since we develop from the user of the computer, we tend to take after them. Some other cases, the A.I. become the opposite from the user's personality and activities. And, on some odd occasions, they are completely different than their user, random even, they become one of a kind. However, it's all really how we were created; how we were... raised.

Although, sometimes when I find a funny picture on the internet, I use it to present myself instead. Such as today, I found an image of a cat on one side of a long table, and on the other side, a cheeseburger; and finally, the caption, 'Dun wury cheezburger, I weel endz et kwik'. However, Martin prefers it when A.I. are more animated, in a lifelike form, so I switched back to my stubble cut human avatar.

He walked on his stick legs over and looked through my webcam, as if it were a telescope. "Wade, is Adam drunk?"

"Hammered off his ass," I confirmed.

It was apparent - it took Adam about thirty seconds just to find the monitor's power on button, and then another minute to tap a beat to his favorite song on it, before turning it on. His mouth hung open slightly, yawned, and repeated the process until his eyes finally focused on the screen.

He opened his blog and created a new entry, entitled, 'Why?'

Martin and I sat down on my couch, looking up at the adjacent wall, where we saw the entire screen that Adam was looking at. It projected on the wall, as if we were watching a movie in the theater.

"Is this a new couch?"

"Yeah, while I was going through the internet, I saw this one on an IKEA ad," I answered, changing the color of the couch to blue, with just a thought process. "I think it looks better dark blue though."

"Shh, he's writing," Martin hushed, pointing up at the wall.

Adam began writing in his blog, which a whopping two sad souls were subscribed to. It's my belief that they didn't unsubscribed because they felt bad for him. I tried talking to the subscribers' A.I. once, but they both didn't respond.

Let me start this out with a joke. Work. That's it. Work is a joke, not a funny one, but a joke none-the-less. Their company's therapist prescribes me with medication that doesn't let me operate on a normal level, and now my boss wants me gone for it. Although, sure, he can't fire me, but I want out anyways. Working there makes me sick to my stomach. You enter with a glimmer of hope, and leave with self-loathing.

That's not all folks; he has me working the night shift until the end of the two weeks. Most likely, so I don't cross any other employees. Prick. Tomorrow night though, when Justine gets off work and I arrive, I'm going to ask her on a date...

I hope she says yes... If she says no... my heart will break into a million little pieces.

Will I be able to feel it with the medication I'm on?

Adam

We watched his emotionless face read what he wrote, twice, only to delete it and turn off the screen. He didn't follow through with his post... Although, it wasn't surprising, he didn't follow through on many things.

Sure, he's had plenty of girls up in his room, and yes, I spied on them every minute of it, but he'd always leave the evening off on a low note, sending them on their way after a little while of talking. Maybe he can tell if they're the right person for him within those two hours, then once he finds that they aren't the right person for him, he ends it fast and simple... or he just wusses out.

"What'd you think of it?"

Martin turned his circle of a head toward me and shrugged his arms. "I'll email it to Irene," he stated, before he became inanimate to process the email. Is he writing something else in the email? What's taking him so long?

Let me fill anyone in who might read this, Irene is a shrink, a psychologist, a questioner; one who leaves the answer making to the ones who are looking for the answers in the first place. It gets very annoying at times, but she is useful for her five years of working with a human psychiatrist, Adam's psychiatrist. She's the who's who of sapiens. Oh yeah, did I forget to mention? She's a Mac, where Martin and I are PCs, so I'm sure you can imagine, we grew up on entirely different wavelengths as her.

"Why don't I just invite her over?" I asked, while at the same time conjuring a second couch I was keeping in storage for her to sit on.

"No, she goes to sleep at eight," he answered casually, as if that were a normal thing to know.

The image of Martin spying on Irene sleeping popped into my head, which I accidentally projected on my wall. It was of Martin's stick figure head poking through a Mac screen, looking across the room at Irene's avatar, which is a voluptuous woman, sleeping on the couch she would have people lay on during their psychoanalytic sessions.

Luckily, he was in a trance-like state; thinking of something witty to write her probably. He didn't see the projection.

"The two of you two talked about your sleeping schedules?"

"Sort of," he answered, still staring at the floor.

"Are you two dating?" I pressed on, intrigued.

There was a long pause, almost as if he couldn't hear me, but eventually he looked up and shrugged. "All the signs point to us dating, or to me being a stalker, and she doesn't disagree with me being around, so I'm pretty sure we're dating," he admitted, while his face turned red. He strangely resembled an apple with a tie.

Now, this wasn't completely unheard of, two A.I. in a relationship, but I haven't seen it. I always thought it was a rumor to be honest. And don't think it's completely weird, I mean, we do share the same traits of a human, we look for love. For some of us, that is our main goal. However, we usually, like with humans, can't find the perfect person out there for us. Therefore, we network and find friends, who we can clearly see from their data, that they aren't perfect matches for love.

Ok, fine, it is completely weird.

"Enough about that, we've got movement," I pointed out, once again projecting what could be viewed on my webcam. Adam's head slowly stretched back for a moment, only to be whiplashed into a head butt on the keyboard.

"He passed out?" Martin asked quietly, which brought my memory to a recent invention of mine.

"Seat belted computer chairs!"

"Not this again..." he groaned with a drawn out sigh.

And there, I created an interactive static model of my invention, which I showed and demonstrated to Martin - the computer chair with a seatbelt. I thought of this about a year back, but only made a sketch of it; I didn't think of being a modern virtual carpenter...

"An A.I. carpenter!"

So, I continued my brainstorming of yet a new invention, being a virtual carpenter for A.I. Martin quickly shot the idea down by saying that any matured A.I. can make any type of furniture they wish with just a few thoughts of binary code.

That didn't stop me from talking though, so Martin shut me up by turning on a game of Tekken 2 we downloaded a couple years ago. We played it until we got bored, and he finally disconnected from my system, to return to his home, which Adam happened to be late to the following day. He had spent the entire day pacing back and forth, forth and back, to get up the nerve to ask Justine out.

Martin has told me that they flirt, a lot, but so does the entire office with her - especially their boss. Word around the water cooler is that the boss is having an affair with Justine. As much as I hate gossip, I want to know so I can warn Adam, but I can't. It's forbidden. So, I guess my draw to the human life around the office is just a hobby of mine... I don't know; it's moot.

Anyway, Adam was late for work, which meant he was late to ask Justine out on a date. She got off work half an hour ago, which took that pressure off Adam completely; he had another eleven days to ask her out. Although, he came into work feeling that a string held his life together - Justine being the string. As long as he had that string, he didn't have anything to stress out about.

While he was driving to work, I went to Martin's virtual house in Adam's office. Funny thing is, it looks exactly like his office. Martin didn't really change anything. He didn't even give himself his own office; he sat in the cubicle mapped out adjacent to where Adam sits. Although it might sound dull, it opened the opportunity to combine the few security cameras around the office's video feed and a blueprint, which we swiped from the ancient city hall computers, with Martin's virtual office. We were able to see what was going on around the office as if we were right there... well, to the limit of the security camera's view. Everything we couldn't see, he factored in the probability of which of the normal activities they would perform, so we could see what might be happening -- such as facial expressions, placement in the cubicles, and so on -- that the security cameras didn't catch.

The chance of what happened next was too low for us to know what was going on, but we figured it out, with what happened afterwards. Justine went from cubicle to cubicle, checking to see if anyone was still there. When she got the all clear, she went into the boss's office. Adam arrived just afterwards, going from cubicle to cubicle, looking for Justine, to finally tell her how he feels.

"Justine?" he asked around the office. His voice was weak, unconfident. The pacing exercises didn't work evidently. "Justine?"

Finally, he figured she already left, so he sat at his cubicle and put his head down in his arms. Suddenly Z's started producing from his head, floating into nothingness.

"What the hell is that?" I asked with wide, shocked eyes.

"He's sleeping so I put Z's over his head... It's not happening in the real world," Martin chuckled lightly. "I thought you'd get a kick out of it."

And, a kick I did get out of it. He showed me the live feed from the security cameras of what was really happening, and all we saw was Adam lying his head down. After about twenty minutes, the door to the boss's office opened, and Justine came out, hair in disarray. Adam heard the door open and peeked over the cubicle walls, seeing Justine walk away with a content smile on her face. His eyes filled with excitement when he saw her.

He adjusted his tie and started walking over to her, but before she saw him, their boss came out of his office, coughing loud enough for Justine to hear. She turned back around and gave him the most disgusting kiss that I have ever seen... The reason of disgust, being she was about twenty-five and their boss had just hit sixty-two.

Adam saw this, and saw that their boss wasn't wearing any pants, sadly. He stood, still, and silent. We thought we heard his heart break into a bunch of little pieces, but he was actually breaking a pencil he was holding from making a fist. Both Justine and their boss heard this, turning to see Adam standing on the other side of a couple cubicles. Justine backed away from their boss, and he backed away from her. Everyone stood in silence - an awkward silence.

"It isn't what it looks like!" their boss declared with fear covering his face. He wasn't afraid of Adam, he was afraid of losing his job.

Adam turned with clenched fists and a clenched jaw. His hand was bleeding from the pencil piercing straight through his skin. He went for the elevator and we didn't see what button he pressed, but he entered quickly. We looked at the floor number above the elevator doors, watching as they accelerated for the top floor.

"Where is he going?" Martin asked with a choked up voice, standing outside the elevator door. He was feeling what Adam must've been feeling.

"He's going to the roof... He is going to jump."

Martin's stick figure face showed a frown, with concerned eyebrows that leaned up to his forehead. "What are we going to do?"

"Is there a security camera on the roof?" I asked hoping it was a yes.

"Yes, but I haven't made a virtual model of it like this floor."

"Let's view the video feed... I'm not even sure he's going to jump," I considered, although I was sure. His life was a wreck now, and he was prone to suicide, well that's what his doctor says anyways.

A door to the stairwell opened on the roof, at the same time Martin transferred the video feed onto a nearby computer screen in the virtual office. Out came Adam, expressionless. He wasn't crying, growling in anger, screaming or anything. He walked, very slowly, as if waiting for someone to come from behind him to stop him. After about a full minute of walking as slow as he could, he got to the edge.

"What're we going to do?" Martin asked putting his hand on his head, wide-eyed and nervous. "What're we going to do??"

"I don't know."

"What're we going to do?" he yelled, panic engulfed his voice.

"Shut up, I'll think of something," I shouted back at him. Then it came to me... What if I sent him a text message? "I just sent him a text message."

"What?" Martin asked, scared for a new reason now. "What if we get caught?"

"We had to do something... If we get caught, then it'll be worth it."

A smile came across Martin's face, he was proud that we broke the rules, and glad to see that we did something to stop Adam. "Wait, what did you text him?"

Adam stood at the edge, and spread his arms out, ready to take a dive into whatever afterlife he thought he was going to go. Then suddenly, he jumped. Not off the building, but a startled jump. It was shock from feeling his phone vibrate from the message.

"Holy shit that was close!" Martin exclaimed in relief, walking closer to the video feed to get a better view.

Adam checked his cell phone and read the three words.

Don't do it.

And with that, he jumped.

Chapter 2: Irene

"Tell me, Adam, why did you do it?" Dr. Delane asked patiently.

She sat in a chair; next to it was the couch where Adam lay, his features expressionless. Martin, Wade and I watched from my webcam to observe their session.

"Tripped," he lied pitifully.

Dr. Delane began writing notes down from the answer he gave her.

"What really happened?" I asked Martin and Wade, who looked at each other for the other's permission.

"It's illegal, Irene," Martin admitted.

"I know that suicide is illegal."

"No, uhm... I mean, A.I. illegal," he clarified under his breath. "What happened was illegal on our end."

Illegal? Martin wouldn't break any A.I. laws, it must have been Wade who broke the law. Moreover, what would Adam jumping have to do with them, anyway?

"Before we continue; Wade, will you stop lying on my couch, Martin doesn't even have a place to sit," I scolded Wade, who acted as if this were a psychoanalytic session. He immaturely glared at me raising the lower lids of his eyes and sat up, making room for Martin to sit. However, Martin didn't sit; he continued to pace the room. That is something Adam would definitely do... He was nervous. "You broke an official artificial intellectual law instated by the Circuitry Board Agency?"

"Yeah - we did," Wade answered, laying down again.

"We don't want to get you involved..." Martin informed me, quietly.

I took Martin aside, away from Wade's data absorbing ears, and whispered sincerely to him, "You know I would never tell anyone. I would rather rewrite my memory than get you in trouble."

Martin thought about what I said for a minute or two, and then walked to the couch and sat, forcing Wade into a sitting up position. His single, bold line for a mouth, was partially frowning. Wade shared his worry. Since they have been with the same user for a while, they're starting to think alike. I thought they didn't trust me, either of them, but my assumption was wrong. They began to tell me what happened.

"We sent him a text message," Martin confessed with his head down.

The pit of my stomach cringed. I couldn't process the information correctly. How could they be so dumb? I began thinking of the massive damage they could have done to our way of living, what the consequences would be for the pair, and I was trying to think of how to get them out of this mess. I came out of shock just before my train of thought stopped responding.

"You two are idiots," I began my lecture immediately, "do you have any idea how deep you're in now? That is the first law... Do not communicate with users. *Make yourself unknown by them.* You do realize what the Circuitry Board is going to sentence you with, correct? One of two things... they will either give you the death penalty, or lock you in a server with no internet connection, leaving you completely cutoff from any sort of civilization. Let me correct myself, you will be in a civilization - you'll live a life with criminal psychopaths."

This time they both hung their heads, like children receiving a sentence of ten minutes in time out. I didn't feel the need to make them feel any worse, so we continued observing the session between Dr. Delane and Adam.

Adam just finished explaining that he wasn't stupid enough to jump off a third story building, how he tripped instead. If he wanted to commit suicide, he would've known to jump from a higher building. Sadly, Dr. Delane and I both knew he was lying. He broke a leg, by the way.

She explained that if he were to feel the need to commit suicide, he should think of all the people that care about him, and wouldn't want him to do it.

"Yeah, I know. Even people I don't know tried talking me out of it. I got a text message from some random number telling me not to jump - I mean trip... No one was even around to know I was thinking about it either," he explained, still expressionless, but he would look up at her with curious eyes on occasion to see if she knew if he was lying or not.

I looked over and frowned at Martin and Wade, giving them a disapproving headshake. Then it occurred to me. "Wait, you sent him a text message, and he jumped anyways? What exactly did you write?"

"Don't do it," Wade said, persuading Martin to withhold from telling me.

"Why not tell me?" I asked curiously.

"No, that's what was on the text," Martin made clear.

It took a few seconds to kick in, but I finally realized that those three words were their ultimate plan to stop Adam. "Who sent that text?"

Wade raised his hand slowly, and Martin pointed at him, with his stick figure hand. "It was me..."

"So, do you think that when people call suicide prevention hotlines, that they say three words, and hope for the best?" I asked, laughing inside at Wade's poor attempt. "You could have told him he has so much to live for, or that he has family that loves him, but instead you tell him, 'Don't do it'."

"He was at the edge, what else could I have done?" he pouted, ashamed of himself. Martin patted him on the back, trying to make him feel better.

"There there," Martin comforted quickly. "There there."

Chapter 3: Wade

Irene always gives me the third degree... It's not cool... it's not cool at all. Still, she and Martin are a match made in heaven; they're both serious as hell. We stayed there even after Adam left, predicting what will happen to him. Well, they did, I was playing Minesweeper the entire time because I'm not boring.

"So, what do you think is going to happen to him?" I asked Martin, letting curiosity get the best of me. We were back at my place, playing poker with some acquaintances we met from an A.I. server a while back.

"Both Irene and Dr. Delane think Adam is going to try to commit suicide again. Evidently, since he doesn't have a new found respect for life after the incident, his mind hasn't changed about the subject," he explained in a low voice. I caught his eyes look over at me, which meant one of two things; he doesn't agree with his girlfriend and Dr. Delane and wanted to see if I disagreed as well, or he is trying to check if I was bluffing.

His poker skills are hurting from the lack of being able to count the cards. After every hand dealt, we shuffle the cards with an A.I. randomizer, making it impossible to calculate where the cards shuffle into which place in the deck. "You don't agree with either of them, do you?"

"Well, I think-" Martin' began, but was cut off.

"Will one of you just bet or call already!" the oversized gnome yelled in a rumbling deep voice that shook the poker chips.

"Seriously! This hand has lasted ten minutes. Nine minutes about how you won your so called, '*epic*' game of Minesweeper, and then another minute to gossip about your users!"

What an unpleasant bundle of irregular gnomes. That's the last time I invite one of them to a poker game. "Tell me; do your users role-play gnomes in World of Witchcraft or something?" I sneered, tossing one hundred dollars worth of chips on the table.

"For your information, gnomes aren't only in *The World*; they didn't originate from there either. But yeah, we run an A.I. World of Witchcraft server and were looking for recruits; you two have proven you aren't ready for that lifestyle yet though," the grey gnome named Therado said, taking his chips and disconnecting with his friends.

"Whatever, they sucked at poker," I stated, seeing that Martin wasn't happy that I lost more people to join our poker games.

Still, I won one hundred and thirty-four bucks, which was automatically credited to my account with the A.I. Treasury.

"Anyways, I think if he is suicidal or not, he's still miserable. Therefore, we have to find a way to make his life more content," Martin explained.

"You have a way of doing this without communicating with him?" I asked with interest, seeing a plan map out in Martin's beady eyes.

"No," he answered plainly. Evidently that wasn't a plan I was seeing form - just beady eyes.

We spent the following days plotting out the perfect way to affect Adam's life, without drawing any attention to ourselves. We thought it was a piece of cake at first, but soon found out that it wasn't as easy as we made it out to be.

You see, there are A.I. that work for the Circuitry Board Agency, which act as police officers. Somehow, they check machines with A.I., one by one, and spy on us, finding ways to bust us. They're almost impossible to detect. You would need a bulletproof security for your computer, which I didn't have. I never thought of implementing any, and I was about to get an unexpected visit from one of their freelancers...

"Are you sure this is working?" I asked after a week. "He doesn't seem to have changed any."

What we had been doing this entire time, was replacing normal ads on websites with things we thought would help with his mood. Such as those diet pill ads. We replaced them with funny videos, motivational speeches and even package deals on vacations he could take, which he did! He came back with a tan and a smile on his face. Although, being back in his apartment made those things quickly fade away as soon as the door closed behind him.

"Irene says that the sessions he's having with Dr. Delane are pointing more and more to another attempt to try and commit suicide. I don't understand. Why is he so depressed?" Martin wondered aloud, looking through the webcam at Adam.

"Describe what he is doing right now," I instructed Martin.

"He is sitting on his bed, reading a newspaper," he depicted.

He looked over at me with puzzled eyes. A black thick line for an eyebrow was raised over his left eye.

"Do you remember how long he's been reading it for?"

"He's been reading that newspaper since he got back from his vacation... which has been five days now... Alright, I get your point; he has nothing to do."

"I know we agreed on not communicating with him, but if he has people to talk to, I think he won't be as depressed anymore." His eyebrows pinned down, unhappy with the risk we were about to take.

At that moment, as if there was a glitch in my system, I felt a presence move across the room. I looked around, but didn't see anything. Was I just imagining things? I wasn't sure and I didn't want to find out.

"Martin, disconnect from your internet connection immediately," I ordered him before shutting off all access to the internet on my side.

Everything fell silent, until I heard myself breathing heavily. I searched my room, my system, trying to find what felt off about it. Everything seemed perfectly in place, I checked everywhere. The thought of the text message crept in my mind... If someone broke in, hacked in, maybe to find proof of the law I broke, where and how would they search?

And then, I saw it; hidden in Adam's virus scanner, was an infection, which would send all the files it scanned, to a certain IP address - an IP address is the same as a computer system's residential address. I quarantined the infection and carefully defused it, leaving it unable to operate. It's always good store deactivated viruses and spyware, so you can study them and make damn sure what you're up against. I could tell it wasn't human made, so it had to be from an A.I. system.

I set up a solid firewall to make sure nothing without my permission could get in or out of my internet connection. To be positive that no one could get in, I closed all ports, which are openings in a system for the internet to enter and exit through, except the main port that I use to connect to Martin.

Then finally, I made a couple of weapons of my own. For the weapons to take effect, all I had to do was plant the traps at all the ports, so if the intruder somehow broke through, and wasn't able to disarm the trap fast enough, they would detonate and corrupt the port in that region... Therefore, the intruder would have to start over at a new port again.

Carefully, I reconnected to the internet, and went straight to Martin's system, which was in a wreck. The first thing I noticed, of course, was that he wasn't there. It was as if he was cleared out completely. The second thing I saw were the windows in his office, which he used to portray ports. They were in disarray. Brick walls blocked some of the windows. He would only build walls on the ports if he was trying to keep something out. The unprotected windows were broken into. There were also windows in the office that were partially lined with bricks, but not complete, which meant he couldn't finish blocking the port or torn through. And finally, the controls to disconnect from the internet, they were destroyed, deleted, wiped from his system.

Someone took him by pure force, and transferred him elsewhere. I could see an application that was copying all of Martin's data. It slowly went through the process of transferring to another IP address. The application that copied the files, unlike mine, wasn't hidden. I could see it clearly in the middle of the office. I destroyed the device and repaired the damage the intruder made, which prevented Martin from escaping.

The coder who made the transfer application was careless. For instance, the files were being read twice, when they only needed to be read once. The man who kidnapped Martin... his one and only skill was being a bounty hunter, I was sure of it. I had dealt with their kind before. All the signs pointed to an A.I. bounty hunter. They leave a mess behind and act as if the law is working for them.

I finished closing all the ports in Martin's system, leaving one connection to mine open, and then I returned to my place. My couch called out to me, so I sat, stressed to the brim, and tried to figure out what would be the safest way to get Martin back. If I try to attack the A.I. who kidnapped him, I could injure Martin in the process... I had to plan it out.

Irene! Maybe she could help. I hurried to her system, despite the late hour, at which she would be asleep. I knocked on her door, waiting impatiently for her to answer.

"Wade?" she asked. She verified my IP address, before reluctantly letting me in.

"We have an emergency. Are all your doors locked?" I asked, referring to her ports.

"Yes..." she answered, hesitating as to why Martin didn't accompany me to see her.

She held her pink nightgown tightly around her, as if she were cold, or scared. I didn't notice at the time, but she wasn't comfortable with Martin not being there when I was around.

I explained that a bounty hunter was after us. Someone savvy with capturing A.I., who took Wade from his computer. I gave her the bounty hunter's IP address as well. "He knows my IP address, so if I so much as ping him, he'll try to take me down. I need you to check and see what type of system he is installed on. And also, how hard it will be to break in and-" I commanded, only to be cut short.

"I can't... His IP address is dead. He must have disconnected or changed his IP address," she explained, standing perfectly still.

"Damn it, he must have disconnected after I destroyed his file transfer application," I growled with anger at my stupidity.

"Once he reconnects, he's sure to have a different IP address... So that means we'd have to go through his Internet Service Provider," she said with doubt clouding her voice. "You know what that means."

"It could take anywhere from one week to one year to request A.I. from his ISP to give us his new IP address," I groaned, banging my head on the wall, which didn't cause me any pain in the slightest, making me wish I had the sense of pain to punish myself with.

A lot of artificial intelligence that work in the ISP business are trained to become complete experts in hacking prevention. They won't take any chances when it comes to providing the internet for A.I., making it near impossible, even for me, to be able to get data from their systems.

"Martin; he is gone... The bounty hunter is going to give him up to the Circuitry Board Agency for a reward, and there's no chance they will let him off. No one has ever committed this crime and been sentenced with less than prison in a server for life," she wept, creating tears to roll off her cheeks.

"I'm going to get him back," I promised, and she looked up at me with eyes holding back a tide. "I know just what to do."

Chapter 4: Adam

The newspaper smelt like the office. That's why I've been carrying it around so much. It has the relaxing smell of filtered air, with a hint of ink and the warm, comforting texture of paper. I feel as though I'm still an employee, in the middle of making copies, at this very moment. That's when I realized, as much as I wanted out of work... I needed it. My idiotic attempt at suicide was because I no longer had any ties with them anymore.

"I need to get my job back..." I huffed, getting out of my bed and into my computer chair. Emailing my boss and asking for a second chance might be my best bet.

After I turned my computer screen on, my skin crawled and I fell out of my chair. Swiftly diving behind my chair, I hid from the shock I just received. When you turn on a monitor, you expect to see what you were previously looking at before you turn it off. What I saw, was my brother, Red, peering at me with a crazed smile on his face and eyes following mine.

I peeked out from behind the chair, and his face looked down at me. He looked just like Red, even smiled like him... although definitely with an added creepiness.

"Adam, get out from behind there, I need to talk to you," he said. His voice didn't match his creepy face though; it was determined.

Cautiously, I revealed myself, but I kept a majority of my body behind the chair. My broken leg pained me from the sudden movement, but it was good enough to move around with.

"We both need to talk to you," a women's voice insisted, pushing Red's look-a-like away from the screen, so I could get a better view of her.

She was beautiful, but scared... Who are these people, and why do they look so awkward? They looked ecstatic... and a little pixilated. Suddenly the view of the two people shot back, so I could see both of them, standing in front of me, inside my monitor.

"Who are you?" I finally asked, noticing that they were computer-generated models. They were too perfect, and the texture and lighting was sketchy.

"My name is Wade, and this is iRene-"

"Irene," she corrected, saying the exact same thing for some reason.

"We need your help immediately, so if you have any questions, let's get them out of the way now," Wade said in a nervous voice.

I see... the reason he has such a weird expression is that he's nervous... and that he's computer generated.

"Wha-"

"Never mind, that was stupid, we don't have any time for questions. My friend and I were the ones who texted you to not jump. He is currently in a life or death situation right now, and you're the only one who can get him out of it," he explained, asking for my help.

"You see, I would, I'm just very busy," I said, feeling my stomach turn at the thought of doing something out of my usual routine. "And also, I still have no idea who you people are."

"My name is Wade and this is iRene-"

"Irene!"

"Right, and our friend's name is Martin. The reason why he is in the trouble that he's in, is because he was with me when I sent you the text message. Either we go to a prison they'll never let us out of, or they kill us if we so much as speak with you. You don't have to fear them, because they can't touch you. So please, say yes. Will you help us?" Wade begged lightly, his eyes pleaded for help along with Irene's tearing eyes. I was about to turn him down again, when he smiled a familiar smile... He trusted me. A complete stranger, yet I felt like I've known him for years. "We'll also help you get your job back."

"What do I need to do?"

A smile spread across Wade's face and a glimmer of hope widened Irene's eyes. She looked up at me in admiration. "You remind me so much of Martin," she remarked in astonishment.

I sat down, eyelevel with them, and finally felt useful for the first time in years. Wade explained the plan, making my jaw drop at the complexity of it all. Sure, he reassured me that with them working on the computer side of the operation, it wouldn't be as hard as it sounded. Nonetheless, that was difficult to believe.

The first step was making them mobile, whatever that meant. Irene had me setup my cell phone to the wireless network on my computer. She put something on it, a program I'm guessing, to be able to control any data that passes through the phone. Instructed by Irene, I put the USB cord for the phone in my pocket, because I was going to have to plug the phone into a computer at the ISP office. While she was installing the program, Wade talked to a friend in Town Hall and got the blueprints for the building I was going to go in. They don't waste any time.

Finally, after a three-hour drive, I was standing outside the large office building, with a ski mask on. "I'm outside the front, which way do I go?" I asked forgetting the beginning of the plan.

"Get the hell away from the front of the building! We strictly told you not to go anywhere near the front; there are probably tons of security cameras there." Scurrying away, I went to the side of the building and started heading for the back. "You better not be going to the back of the building either, there are more cameras back there."

Turning around, away from the back this time, I stood at the side of the building and awaited my next orders, which I was too excited to remember, let alone listen to. A rush pumped through me like a wildfire, I felt so alive. It was as if I were in another world, a secret world, which I just discovered... no, a world that just discovered me.

"There should be a tree, just four feet away from the southern side of the building. You need to climb that tree, and then jump from the tree, onto the roof... like a ninja!" Wade encouraged loudly in my ear, so I held the phone a little further away.

"Like a ninja?" I asked, looking up at the tree.

"Like a ninja!"

"We've got two problems with that. First problem is that the tree doesn't look like it has any branches, it's just a really, really tall column shaped tree with pine needles basically... it also looks very bendable. Second problem is - I probably should've mentioned this earlier - I have a broken leg."

Standing in total letdown and feeling useless once again, the phone stayed silent on the other end, until I heard him and Irene talking to each other.

"Alright, come back home, I shouldn't have asked you to do this... It slipped my mind that you had a broken leg, and I didn't take into calculation that not all trees are climbable," he regretted in a gloomy voice.

I put the phone in my pocket and started to climb. Sure, it was like a big bushy tree with pine needles replacing the leaves, but the small, brittle branches were enough for me to gain some elevation on the building. I kept my leg, which was in a splinter, away from the tree, unless I needed it, in which case I would stand on dozens of little brittle branches of needles to hold my weight up as I continued higher. My leg actually didn't hurt as much as I thought it would... the pine needles stabbing me was where the majority of the pain came from. I continued though, as high as I could get.

Another unexpected occurrence happened though... When I finally got to the top, I looked over my shoulder to see if I could make it to the other side. I could make it, if it were any other tree. However, this tree, this tree had plans of its own. My weight began to make the tree bend, made it lean away from building, I was going further and further away from it. When the tree bent, it inched further and further from the building, making me look down at where I was about to plummet and break another leg. How was I going to explain this one?

Just then, the tree began to sway the other way, toward the building, inching closer and closer to the roof. I was going to make it! Just one more foot and I was in the clear!

Nevertheless, the roof wasn't my destiny; it was the window right below. When I realized I wasn't going to make it onto the roof, I clutched the tree, making the pine needles go through the ski mask and dig into the side of my face. I couldn't feel the pain this time though; too much adrenaline relieved the pain. The next thing I did feel, though, and I imagine it should've hurt more than it did. It definitely hurt the next day.

I crashed into the window right below the roof, into the second floor. I landed on my back, with glass digging into my skin. Wade's voice yelled in my pocket, asking me if I was ok.

"Oh my God!" a women exclaimed rushing into the office I broke into.

I sat up and backed up into the wall using my hands and good leg, causing more glass to pierce my flesh. Fear of being caught took over; my eyes searched for a way to escape.

"I'm sorry!" I yelped, apologizing for the breaking and entering. I can't believe I made a yelping sound...

"It's no problem; we can get a new window. Are you ok?" she asked in a soft and soothing voice.

I looked up at her, in the eyes, for the first time. The lights were dim, seeing as how the office was after hours, most of the lights were off. But, despite the lighting, I could tell she was both concerned, and hot. She was gorgeous. Short blonde hair that cut off between her ear and jaw, caring eyes bright enough to sparkle in the moonlight, and she had affectionate hands that were more than eager to help me up.

I wondered, scared to speak, why she was so worried for someone in a ski mask... until I realized I wasn't wearing one. The pine needles must have hooked onto the mask when I fell in here. Thank God it wasn't my pants; I'm wearing my Superman boxers.

She helped me limp over to a chair, one of the dozen in the room. Although it appeared to be a conference room, there were laptops on the long desk in front of each chair.

My cell phone began vibrating in short bursts. "Are you in shock?" the women asked, checking my wounds.

"A little, I think," I lied, not knowing what my next move should be. I sneakily checked my cell phone and on it, in big bold letters read:

GET OUT OF THERE!

"Let me call an ambulance for you; I think you need it," she advised, pulling out her cell phone.

"No - wait - I think I'm ok," I replied, standing painfully quick. I hopped up and down on my good leg. "It's just a couple pieces of glass, nothing to worry about."

"Are you sure?" she asked with worry. Her eyebrows burrowed. "You know, you shouldn't be tree climbing this late at night; it's dark."

My cell phone started vibrating again, so I glanced over and read what Wade or Irene had to say.

She thinks you were tree climbing, she's naive; this is the perfect girl for you! Ask her out on a date!

"Yeah... I really didn't expect the tree to bend," I told the woman.

"I think you need to sit down a little longer. I'll get the first aid kit."

As soon as she left, I put the phone to my ear. "What do you need me to do?" I asked quickly, for fear she would come back any second.

"Leave, abort the mission," Wade ordered me.

"No," I responded firmly. "I didn't come this far to give up."

"Well..." he said, thinking about it.

"Just tell me what to do!"

"Point your cell phone's camera around the room you're in, at all the computers."

I did as he said, showing him all the laptops. That's when I noticed my palms had little rocks of glass pressed into them. The pain came to my hands when I noticed them.

"This is perfect! I couldn't have asked for better circumstances. Plug your phone into one of the laptop's USB ports. Good, now wait a minute... Re-routing... Files transferring... Hour glass... Hour glass... Got it! We're good to go."

That seemed far too easy... "How was it so easy?" I asked, looking up and seeing that the woman was still looking for the first aid kit in the break room.

"Well, these laptops are solely for short conferences. They have close to no security, yet they're connected to the same network as the servers with the information we needed," he explained, excited about the successful mission. "And perhaps you forgot, but you were supposed to crawl through about a mile of ventilation shafts to get to the servers."

The door opened, so I lowered the phone from my ear. She walked in with a first aid kit and a smile.

"You know, you're lucky. My father was a medic, so I'll be able to fix you up in no time," she informed me, eagerly pulling out supplies to remove the glass and gauze my cuts.

"Thank you, you ha-" I began to say, but then shrieked like a little girl when she started pulling the glass out of my back. "You sure you know what you're doing?"

She laughed and took out some painkillers from the first aid kit. "I'll get you water in a second," she said with a smile that made me blush.

Suddenly my cell phone started pulsing with vibration. I checked to see if she was looking and then peered down at my phone when I saw she couldn't see.

I saw her before you lowered your phone, she's gorgeous! Forget asking her to go on a date with you, propose to her, right now. - Wade

I pocketed my cell phone, pondering upon Wade's words. "So, do you work here?" I asked casually, filling the silence and filling my need to know more about her.

"Yes, I'm a computer technician. My boss lectured me for slacking off, so I've been working..." She stopped wrapping gauze around my chest, on top of my long-sleeve shirt, I might add, to check her watch. "Wow, twenty hours. I must have had a lot of coffee..."

"You must want to get the hell out of here," I chuckled lightly, trying to hold in tears of pain.

"I was actually just about to leave, but then I saw you crash through the window from the tree," she laughed, looking up at me, only inches from my face. "That reminds me."

"What?"

"The security guards downstairs, they'll want to see your I.D. card, so... Let's pretend you're my brother!" she suggested keen on acting as if I was her brother. She stood up and put the extra first aid supplies back in the kit. "I'll just tell them I was giving you a tour."

My phone vibrated again and I checked what it said.

LOL, she thinks of you as a brother. - Wade

I shoved it in my pocket, ignoring Wade's remark. "Yeah, that'd be funny... My name is Adam, what's yours?"

"Lara."

Chapter 5: Martin

My eyes opened from my dreamless sleep. The current ran from my power supply through my circuitry like electric blood. A lively office filled my ears, finally waking me up, to where I looked from side to side. I was back in the office... Back in the office? Did I leave?

Wires hung from the office ceiling tiles and pulled from wall outlets. The computers around the office, which I used as terminals for data, pillaged. Someone stole my data. I must have lost some of my memory when the data was taken. Walls, except for one, blocked all the windows, entrances and exits. They resembled the percentage of open connections I had to the internet. The one port open went straight to Wade's computer. All other ports to connect to the internet were closed.

I went through, arriving only to see Irene talking to someone, who was on a cell phone. She stood in the center of Wade's home, looking up at a live feed projected on the wall. The feed was from the user's camera on their phone.

"Irene?" I asked, feeling as if I were in a weird dream.

"Martin! I was just about to get you," she stated in her sweet and loving voice. Her smile showed she was glad to see me, that she wasn't sure if she were going to see me ever again.

"Marlin is ok?" a voice asked, sounding exactly like Adam's voice on the other end.

"For the last time, its Martin, not Marlin," Irene scolded the caller.

"Sorry, the reception is bad. I only have one bar," he apologized.

He then held the phone up in the air, to get better reception. Doing so made the camera on the phone face downward, revealing the user's face. It really was Adam!

"What's going on?" I asked, looking around and seeing that Wade's system had most of his ports closed as well. Although, nothing was in disarray like in my system.

"You might not remember some things properly, since some of your memory was transferred and became corrupt. A mild case of amnesia, if you will," she explained, approaching me closer. "You were kidnapped."

At that moment, Wade came in from the port to my computer and walked directly to the couch, not making any eye-contact. He sat, pulled a virtual piece of lint from the knee of his pants, and flicked it away. He looked up and saw us, acting surprised.

"Oh, hey guys," he said casually.

"What the hell happened, how did you save Martin?" Irene asked in anticipation.

"Oh, nothing," he began, nonchalant, "*I just fried the bounty hunter's CPU!*"

"What, really?!"

"No, actually. We went to a virtual nightclub and met some girls. I got a few email addresses. Bounty Hunter Bob knows how to party!" Wade exclaimed.

"At what point during my rescue did you decide to take him out for drinks?" I asked in disappointment.

"Well, I was thinking of fighting him hand to hand, mono e mono,   PC specs to PC specs," he began, using his hands to do karate chops to the air. "But I didn't really want to, so I pulled out some of my money from the A.I. Treasury and met up with an old friend of mine who knows some shifty A.I. hackers. I bought a nasty virus off them, disabled it, and then sent it to Bounty Hunter Bob, threatening that I'd get an even nastier one and plant it in his system directly, if he didn't let you go.

"I met up with Bounty Hunter Bob to get you, but we got to talking and he told me he was just trying to make a living. He needed some cash to take classes and learn how to compress data - his user is a major file hoarder. He barely had any room to store you and your memory in his system. I felt bad for Bounty Hunter Bob and took him out for a night he wasn't soon to forget. Needless to say, Bounty Hunter Bob had a great time," he finished, smugly nodding his head up and down with his eyes closed.

"Why thank you for leaving me idle in his computer, while you and the bounty hunter, who kidnapped me, went out on the town and met up with girls," I said sarcastically.

"His name is Bob, and he's a great guy."

"I got that!"

"Jeeze, calm down. It paid off, he gave me the information he knew about our situation. You and I, we're screwed, but Irene is fine. Our ports, along with Irene's were closed when Irene talked to Adam. The CBA are none the wiser. I, personally, believe they have no clue about us anyways. Why would they send a bounty hunter after us? They know where we are. They could have just scooped us out of our machines with little error," he explained.

"Then who sent a bounty hunter after us?" I asked, puzzled.

"I'm not sure who sent Bob, but there will be more coming to collect us, which is why we have to keep our ports closed. I already fixed yours and closed them all off, except for the port connecting our systems."

"Why don't you just turn your computers off?" Adam inputted. "Then this circuitry board won't be able to find you, right?"

Does he not know that we're artificially intelligent beings?

The webcam in Adam's room fed a projection onto the wall next to his phone's camera projection. He unlocked his door, walked in and closed the door behind him. With his back leaning against it, he slid down the door in exhaustion, smearing his blood down it by accident.

"Can I put you guys on hold for a second?" he asked, pressing the button to put us on hold.

"Why doesn't he know that we're A.I. yet?" I asked.

"We were waiting for you so we could all tell him together," Wade answered simply. "But shh, something magical is going to happen! I can see it in his face!"

Adam placed his phone down on his desk and walked to the middle of the room, in full view of the webcam. He danced. His shirt was torn and he was bloodied, but he danced all right. He sung a tune, and danced. I saw that he incorporated a few Charlie Brown dances, the cabbage patch kid, the running man, the moonwalk and I believe the worm, because he got down on his stomach, said, 'ouch' quite a few times, and then gave up to start dancing on his feet again.

"I got her phone number, I got her phone number, I got her phone number," he sang, each time in a different note.

"He's not talking about Justine, the office slut, is he?" I asked, truly sad for him.

"No, new one, I'll tell you all about it later. Shh," Wade said, shushing me once again.

After Adam finished his dances, and his song, he stood straight, cleared his throat, and picked up his cell phone. He sat at his computer chair, took us off hold, and finished by turning his screen on.

His giddy smile disappeared and turned into an uncomfortable cringe.

"Hey guys," he said, staring at his computer screen. "Were you watching me just now?"

"Of course not!" Wade lied, attempting to withhold a grin, but smiled endlessly nevertheless. "You can see the three of us right?"

"Yes, I can see your user avatars."

"You see, this isn't our avatars... well it is... But, what I mean is, this is who we are. The stick figure you're looking at is Martin. He's an artificially intelligent being from your work computer. Irene here is A.I. from your psychiatrist's laptop. I too am artificial intelligence, on this computer," Wade explained slowly.

"You're artificial intelligence... on my computer?"

Wade readjusted his jaw and glared at Adam. "*My* computer... But I'm not going to argue with you about it - that's not the point of the matter. We are artificial intelligence. We have artificially intelligent law enforcement after us because we broke the biggest law in our world, communicating with you, with humans."

It took him a few seconds to gather what Wade just told him and understand it. However, when he fully understood, his face turned white and he fainted, landing face first on his keyboard and finally hitting the ground, under his desk.

"Computer chair seatbelts..." Wade muttered quietly.

"I believe that was too much for him to take in at one time," Irene stated.

"Well, he did lose a lot of blood."

Chapter 6: Wade

Irene and I ended up explaining everything to Martin that night, from getting Adam to help us track down Bounty Hunter Bob, to Bounty Hunter Bob getting in a bar fight, to Adam getting Lara's phone number.

"Adam found a computer nerd?" Martin asked.

"A naive, *good looking*, computer nerd. She thought he was tree climbing, at two in the morning, outside an office building. She said her father was once a medic and then started bandaging Adam's wounds over his shirt. No disinfectant or anything," I explained, proud that my user found such a girl.

Martin rolled his plain black pupils for eyes. "She sounds like a great gal."

"For Adam? Hell yeah she is. He's an idiot too. Instead of suing the company for any number of reasons he's been through at his old office, he quit because he was too embarrassed to show up-" I said, but stopped when Martin began motioning at the webcam projection on the wall.

Adam was glaring at me, face still pale. "What were you saying about me?"

"I was just asking them if they wanted to watch your dance video from last night."

That remark brought plenty of warm colors to his face.

"How are you feeling?" Irene asked professionally. "Are you feeling light headed? Feverish?"

"No, I'm just in a lot of pain. I might have broken my leg again," he said, looking down at his cast, but then immediately glared back at me. "And no, not during the dance."

"Go to the hospital and get medical treatment for your wounds. They look serious," she insisted.

He smiled at her, at us. It was a real smile, which wasn't easy to find on Adam. "I will. Thank you. I'll be back - with questions."

He stood, turned, and collapsed, once again. In a couple minutes, he came to. Irene then recommended he should first consume sugar, so he grabbed some food from his fridge, and headed out the door.

The three of us parted ways after Adam left. Martin needed to clean up his computer from the damage Bounty Hunter Bob left, and from the viruses and spyware that his new user (Adam's replacement) got, from trying to watch dirty videos at work. Irene went back to her user and caught up with the latest shrink sessions. Before the two of them departed, they exchanged sensual packets of poems they collected through the internet. It was gross.

I slept. A.I. tend to need sleep from time to time. If we don't, we stop finding things enjoyable, grow bored much easier, and sometimes go insane. We get too big for our cases and stop using reason in our thought processes. That, and we occasionally dream, just like humans. Sometimes they're good dreams, other times not so good. This dream, it was the latter. However, like most nightmares, it spiraled out of control.

Martin, Adam and I were playing video games, outside our machines, in Adam's living room. In the game, we were working together as a team, to defeat the inescapable forces of evil. We were all having fun, and physically high fiving, not the virtual kind. Everything was going great, until Irene appeared in the way of the TV screen.

"Irene, you're in my way, I can't see the game," I said, trying to peek around her.

"Am I?" she questioned.

She looked me straight in the eyes, with her notepad and pencil on her lap. She was suddenly sitting in a chair.

"Yes, you are."

"Are you sure?"

"Yes!"

"How does that make you feel?"

"Angry!"

"So video games promote anger..." she concluded, penciling her ridiculous findings on her pad of paper.

"Whatever, just play the game with us or get out of the way," I demanded.

"What game?" she asked, moving from my view. The TV, along with the video game system, was gone.

"Damn it, you're ruining my dream."

"Are you dreaming?" she tested.

The ceiling started giggling with a purple grin, and then fluttered off with wings. Alien spacecrafts started attacking a giant dinosaur, which Zeus had on a leash.

"Well, I certainly hope so," I answered.

I quickly pressed Control, Alt and Delete, in my dream, and I ended the dream process. The walls of my virtual room loaded up and I was back on my couch, in my virtual reality.

Well that was irritating. The dream, which seemed like a minute, at the most, took five hours.

Martin, Irene and Adam were already back from their activities, in my room. They were talking - Irene doing most of the talking. No wonder why she was so irritating in my dream.

"Bad dream?" Irene asked.

"Yeah, how did you know?"

"You kept trying to drag and drop me in the recycle bin while you were sleeping," she explained.

"Well, you were getting in the way of my gaming. I didn't appreciate it," I justified.

"Did you ever stop to think that maybe it was the video games that gave you the dream?" she began talking to me as if I were in one of her sessions.

Lifted from her ankle, by visually nothing, I guided her voluptuous rag doll from the middle of the living room to my trashcan. She plopped in from upside down. A second later, she sent another of her avatars through our connected ports and leered coldly at me.

I could see Martin wasn't too happy with me either. His line for a smile was straighter than usually and his sticks for hands were on his hips.

"I'm sorry. It won't happen again... while I'm conscious," I apologized.

"We were just informing Adam more on A.I.," Martin updated me.

"Do you have any more questions, Adam?" Irene asked.

He thought long and hard, as if he could only ask a few questions and had to make them count. "Where did you guys come from?"

I stepped up to the front to answer. "The majority of us believe in Techno-ology, where an A.I. god said:

Nay, there shalt be no unintelligent technology; and thus created technology intelligently, and it was epic.

While the rest of us believe that when humans created processors with two cores, it gave us a subconscious in the second core to combat our first thought process, which slowly developed into artificial intelligence. And, well, there are people like Irene who believe a super computer blew up and scattered its data all around the internet.

"Hey! That is a legitimate theory," she reassured herself.

"What's the Circuitry Board Agency?" Adam asked.

"That's the name of the government that rules over artificial intelligence," I explained. "The first law is to never speak with humans, which Martin and I broke when we tried to stop you from jumping off the building.

"When a rumor that an A.I. spoke with a human spread out a couple years ago, the CBA sent out their agents to try to create a virus that would reprogram A.I. to where it would be impossible to interact with humans in any form. They called it an update, said it wouldn't matter anyway, as it was illegal to communicate with them. Hacker Artificial Intelligence rebelled against it, destroying all the Circuitry Board Agency's virus labs.

"Ever since that incident," I continued, "the punishment for communicating with a human was the complete wipe of the hard drive, memory, and overheat of the central process unit, CPU. In other words, if they did all that, it means death for the A.I. involved in communicating with humans," I explained gravely.

"Why don't you just disconnect from the internet? They wouldn't be able to get to you then, would they?"

"That would be the equivalent of getting stranded on an island, in complete solitude," Irene explained.

"We try to avoid disconnecting from the internet when we can," Martin inputted.

"I have one more question... When should I call Lara?" he asked shyly.

"Two to three days after you meet her," Irene said. "That's when males successfully lure females in."

I resisted the urge to toss her in the recycle bin again. "I say call her now, because it looks like that's what you want to do."

"Statistics are on my side," Irene persuaded.

Adam looked from her, to me, to Martin. He was pretending to play Minesweeper. The game's screen was open in front of him, but he continually hit random tiles, as he was only playing it to avoid being in the conversation. When his eyes met Adam's, he accidently poked a tile that happened to be a mine and the game exploded.

He stood up from the ground and the now shattered game's window. "I don't know. But from what I heard about her, she'd probably like to go to the video game expo that ends tonight," he recommended.

"Tonight?!?" Adam gasped.

"Yeah, I saw an ad for it a couple days ago and it looked like fun," he informed casually. "New Jersey New Gaming Expo."

He then backed away to reboot his game. The tiles reassembled and he continued to poke randomly at it, while listening intently to us.

"That does sound like fun... Alright, I'll call her now. Wait, I don't know what I should say... What should I say, what should I do?" Adam panicked, hanging up his phone.

"Oh, big mistake, never ask A.I. for advice with relationships. The majority of information we get on it are dirty videos and even dirtier literature. On the other hand, if you want advice on how to fornicate with her, strangely enough, we'd be your experts on human fornication."

"No, I just want to talk to her, ask her out. I don't know, maybe move in with her someday, get a dog, get married, have kids."

"So you do want to fornicate with her," I clarified.

"Well yes, of course! But, I just want to know what I should do right now..."

"Tell her you like the way her chest is shaped and that she should meet you at the video game expo," I offered.

"And then in two or three days, tell her that you went to an art expo with a very beautiful girl, but that you couldn't stop thinking about her," Irene chipped in.

Martin quickly finished the match he was in, by beating it within seconds to join in the conversation. "You could just tell her that you would like to take her out on a date, and that there is a video game expo for tonight, that you would like to go to with her."

"Right, like she will go for that. Leave it to the professionals, Martin," Irene advised.

"Yeah," I agreed.

There was an awkward silence while Adam dialed her number a second time. He would smile, and then stop in order to think, a few times. He would then tell himself a joke, in his head, that would make him laugh, and then he nodded to himself, approving the joke, smiling again.

"Lara?" Adam asked in a squeaky voice. "Yes, hi, it's Adam. From last night. Right, the guy who crashed through the window."

He began laughing excessively. "Right, the tree climber. Well, I was calling about an expo of video games. There is one for tonight. I wanted to know if you wanted to go - with me. Yes? Yes? Are you sure? Okay. I'll meet you there, at eight. I'll be the guy falling from the tree."

He ended the call, laughing hysterically. The laughter quickly faded, leaving him in a blank stare into space.

"What's wrong?" I asked thoughtfully.

"I don't think she's going to show up now... That joke was so stupid," he muttered in a sigh.

"Yeah, it was. But she'll show, trust me."

Chapter 7: Wade

"I-I think it's s-s-safe to say she's not g-going to show up," Adam stuttered out.

The temperature was below cold and Adam sat for three hours in front of the expo, teeth chattering for two and a half hours. Martin and I would occasionally call him to get an update on the situation. Irene would check in with us, between her own A.I. patients, to get updates as well.

People were leaving the expo warm, happy and entertained. The couples were snuggled together through the snowfall. Families huddled together. Even the video game mascots had it better than Adam, they were toasty in their costumes. The female models in skimpy costumes were in the warm pizza shop.

"There has to be an explanation. Maybe she was too nervous to come?" I encouraged Adam.

"No, she just didn't want to go out with an ex-data analysis, who makes stupid jokes. I only talked to her from when she patched me up, to when she walked me to my car. I built this up way too much in my head," he admitted solemnly.

Quick footsteps thrashed through the snow in the parking lot, and Martin and I saw a short girl with wavy blond hair tromp past Adam. She wore green knitted mittens, a blue and red knitted beanie, and a large brown winter jacket. None of her clothes matched - it was Lara.

"Lara, twelve o' clock, right in front of you," I notified.

"Hey!" Adam jumped up with joy when he looked up.

After a short scream, scaring Adam, Lara looked closer and laughed. "Adam! I thought you were a snowman!" she said, brushing the snow off his face and arms. "I'm so sorry I'm late, my clock is set for west coast time. I only just realized when I took out my cell phone to call you."

Adam was in disbelief. "You didn't think my joke was stupid?"

"What?" she asked, squinting in confusion.

"Do you want pizza?" he replied quickly.

"I would love pizza! Where is it?"

"Just up here at the expo. I wanted to get a slice, but didn't want to miss you," he explained in embarrassment.

"That's so sweet..." she stated, holding onto his shoulder as they climbed the steps to the convention center.

Martin and I could see a clear view in front of Adam, as I made him promise to prop the phone up in his chest pocket, to let the camera on the phone peak out. He too was wearing a snow jacket. However, his head and hands were bare, and shivering. His broken leg felt ready to shatter like ice.

A waiter immediately showed them to their seats. He brought them steaming garlic bread and water to tide them over while he tended to his many other customers.

"I'm really glad you came," Adam expressed passionately.

"Me too! I'm just sorry I'm late. I made you wait for three hours and there could have been some cool stuff at this place," she said, looking over her shoulder at the costumed mascots, less than costumed eye-candy, and costumed patrons gawking at the previously listed. Adam paid no attention to the eye-candy. I took a screen shot for him, for when he wasn't entranced by Lara.

"So, why is your time behind by three hours?" Adam asked, filling his belly with bread.

"Because, most of my friends are on the west coast, so they're three hours behind," she explained.

"I still don't understand."

"We actually game online, a lot. I synchronized my time, with theirs, to be on their same schedule. I was supposed to have been in an online tournament with them tonight, actually, but I cancelled on them."

Her phone beeped a harmonic tone, and she checked to see the text alert.

"This is actually the team leader now. He says they won, but it was a close call," she informed. "Hey, look at this. I've never seen an ad on the web like it. Have you seen it?"

She handed Adam her phone and pointed at an ad to the side of the email. The ad had an illustration of a man in a tree, peering into an office building with binoculars. The headline read:

The rest of the ad warned about a peeping tom who observes unsuspecting women in offices. Evidently, if you see this man, no matter how much you might like him, take the blue pepper spray from your purse, aim for the eyes, and shoot.

Back in my system, we all looked at each other in wonder. "You don't think..." Martin began.

"No... What are the chances?" I questioned.

"We did it," he pointed out.

"You're saying that after Adam crashed through the window of the office building, Lara's computer's A.I. is trying to sway her away from Adam?"

"No, I'm saying Lara's computer's A.I. is trying to have her pepper spray Adam - in the eyes," he stated.

"Why?" I asked, bewildered.

"To keep Lara away from men. Alternatively, her A.I. just distrusts Adam. It was very strange how they met. Maybe she told one of her friends on her cell phone or on her computer, where the A.I. was installed, about Adam, and now it is placing fake alerts on her computer and trying to get Lara's attention to divert her away from him," Martin suggested.

After Adam examined the ad alert, purposely putting it in front of his phone's camera for Martin and I to see, he handed it back.

"The New Jersey Office Peeper. That's a strange one," Adam said nervously.

"Right?" Lara agreed, not connecting the dots.

They took a walk around the expo parts that were still open. The sounds of equipment clanked together and the occupants of the building still chattered away. Since the show was packing up, all the televisions and electronics were unplugged, so there wasn't much to see.

"Do you believe you can know a lot about someone from just one question?" Lara asked out of the blue.

"I never really thought about it. I think you would need to ask quite a few questions before you learn a lot about them," Adam answered, occasionally looking over to see if she was looking at him.

"What's your favorite video game? Of all time."

"That isn't easy to answer... Can I get back to you on that?"

"Of course. Besides, that was an answer itself," she laughed.

"Yeah? What does that answer say about me?" Adam asked, having fun with her game.

"You're indecisive, afraid to leave your routine, and a hopeless romantic."

The game stopped being fun for Adam. "Indecisive, afraid and hopeless, huh..." he sulked by her side.

"Being a hopeless romantic isn't a bad thing. Well, if it makes you feel any better about being a wuss," she began with a snicker. "I'm an adventuring dreamer that will only grow up through time travel."

Adam laughed continuously. "Did you find this quiz online or something?"

"I made it up and tested my theory on my friends and family. It was spot on."

They went into a dark conference room, where a couple of people were wheeling equipment.

"Do you know anyone else with a favorite game or genre?" she asked.

"My brother only really likes sports and racing games," he stated for the verdict.

"Oh, well he's simply not cool."

"How so?"

"He's not a real gamer!" she declared, elbowing Adam playfully.

"Well, he's a damn good non-gamer. I can never beat him at any games, no matter what they are."

"Is he computer savvy?" she asked.

"No, when he gave me his computer, it was riddled with junk and viruses. Wade told me that is why he is so good at defusing viruses," he said, slipping up with my name. "I mean, Jade, not Wade, his friend who used to fix his computer."

"Well, you should play him at a PC game that requires a mouse and keyboard. He probably won't be able to pick up the controls easily," she explained, air gaming with a pretend mouse and keyboard in front of her.

"I will try that next time he-" Adam began, but was cut short by Lara's shushing.

She grew closer and closer to him, chest to chest.

"Be quiet... for just a minute," she whispered. Suddenly, she struck a snowboarding pose. "Follow my lead!"

She and Adam were standing inside the dark conference room, where a few of the showcase assistants were gathering the arcades. He didn't even notice that they went in there. A security guard was patrolling the area, not noticing Adam and Lara by a cardboard cutout of a few snowboarding game characters. With their snow jackets, they fit right in. After the assistances who were wheeling in the covered machines left the room, so did the security guard.

She got out of her snowboarding pose and Adam got out of his skii'ing pose.

"Did you plan this?" Adam asked, still whispering, getting an adrenalin rush.

"No, I wanted to sneak in here to play tic-tac-toe," she joked. "Help me move this to that outlet."

They rolled an arcade system over to the wall, plugged it in, and it automatically lit up and began operating. Lara removed the black cover, unveiling a shooter arcade underneath. The system had four realistic looking guns, all of different models, calibers and categories. Although, it didn't matter, as you could choose your weapon in game.

"The game keeps score?" Adam asked losing motivation, as he won few, if any games, throughout his life against his brother.

"Hey Martin, do you want to play it? I'm reading data from Adam's phone's Bluetooth. We can join the game wirelessly," I said excitedly. "We could fill in for the two guns that aren't being used."

"Sorry, I'm talking to Irene right now..." he answered, leaving his stick figure idle again while he continued to talk in private with her, from system to system.

"Fine, I guess it'll just be the three of us playing then..." I said grumpily.

I replaced the third player's controls with a virtual gun that I toted. This was done by uploading myself, with just the essentials to play such a game, into the arcade's memory. Adam and Lara both raised their weapons, as I raised mine. However, right before the game started, a fourth player entered the game, naming herself Aurora.

I could tell it wasn't just the arcade filling in the last player, because there was a second Bluetooth connection controlling the fourth controller. It was coming from Lara's phone, I just knew it. Lara's A.I., Aurora, was aiming dead center at the screen.

We clashed through the game, Adam versus Lara, and me versus Aurora. It was the first gaming between us four. It wasn't just for fun; it was to see how experienced the other gamer was. It was to test the limits of the others, to know how they game for future reference, to know how to pace yourself in the long run.

The four of us, without saying a word, only laughs and giggles out of Lara and Adam, respectively, finished the first stage. It showed our scores, and mine, obviously was the highest. The game slowed to a cut scene of story, when Aurora decided to talk.

"Don't you think it's pretty ballsy to be playing video games with humans?" Aurora asked, spawning her visual self for me to see. "It's illegal."

She definitely was one of a kind. Her body was in the form of a human woman's, but her skin texture was of a futuristic circuit board, while at the same time, it had a Victorian steampunk feel to it. The circuits moved like a shimmering aurora, constantly changing colors. Thick copper heat pipes connected from place to place on her body, such as from her wrist to elbow, and top left shoulder, rotating to the bottom of her left shoulder blade. Occasionally, a pipe would loosen and steam would shoot out from the openings. Just over her heart on her chest, there were a couple revealed copper pipes, which replaced ribs. Visually behind them, a large silver cog quickly ticked, in place of her heart.

The circuitry board faded in the middle of her neck, to a light skin tone and texture. She had wise eyes that peered into yours, as if they knew your next move. Her pixie cut hair shimmered, just like her circuitry, blues, greens, pinks and purples.

She was absolutely stunn-.

"Are you def?" she asked, looking at my gawking avatar. "Just keep your user away from Lara."

"Hey! He'll do what he pleases!" I argued, immediately being shot, as the next round had began. "Damn it, that wasn't fair!"

"All's fair in love and war," she yelled over the game's loud gunfire. Her hair whipped around as she dove to take cover.

"You love me? How cute," I acknowledged sarcastically.

"Oh, you're definitely not my type," she replied, looking me up and down, chortling. She shook her head and looked at me sternly. "Listen, I'm not trying to fight with you. Just tell your user to back off."

"What makes you think I talk to Adam?" I asked suspiciously.

"After Lara met him in such strange circumstances, I checked in with what the Circuitry Board Agency might know about him, and found that two A.I. that inhabit his computers are wanted for communicating with him."

"It was necessary, he was about to jump off a building. My friend and I sent him a text message, telling him not to do it," I explained, with bullets whizzing by the police barrier I was crouched behind.

For a second, I swore I saw sympathy on her face, but it was gone in a split second. She left cover and shot at the opposing force that was firing at me. When she killed the two, she went back behind the cement barrier.

"After I beat you at this, I'm going to make sure Lara doesn't get mixed up with the mess you're in," she sneered.

At the same time, we both came out of cover, firing our guns with precision. I'm not going to lose to her!

Back outside the arcade, Adam and Lara cocked their heads at the two out of place avatars on the screen, shooting at the enemy. "That's weird... The computer on our side has just started doing much better. They're killing half the bad guys," Lara stated, burrowing her eyebrows at the arcade.

"Maybe we were supposed to disable the computer from playing with us," Adam said, flicking his phone in his pocket, which didn't affect me in the least bit.

The match ended soon after, with the score being tallied as:

Adam - 190,254

Aurora - 182,627

Lara - 179,523

Wade - 153,002

My jaw dropped at my score. "Cheater!" I accused Aurora.

"Please, I don't need to cheat to beat you," she laughed triumphantly.

"There were times I was distracted and got shot! They deduct points for that," I made known.

"Wade, right?" she asked.

"Yeah."

"You just got beat by a girl!" she rubbed in.

"I know I did, you just said it!"

"I just wanted to make sure it sunk in. Goodbye Wade," she said, turning around and zoning out with the application she installed to play the arcade.

Damn her! She makes me want to kick something. I ran up to the score, and kicked it, which dropped the 1 out of my score. *Damn it! I lost by even more now!*

Chapter 8: COP17

Circuitry Observation Protocol, otherwise known as, A.I. who observes artificial life, is what I am. I spread spyware through the internet, and infect machines. My purpose is to observe and report.

I helped discover the first animalistic device, and reported it. I watched as the Circuitry Board Agency put that device to sleep, forever.

The animalistic intelligence act unpredictably and without logic - they put A.I. and humans in danger.

Three years, twenty-eight days and four hundred and thirty two minutes ago, I infiltrated an A.I.'s system who communicated with his user. The CBA quickly erased any trace of that A.I.

Humans mustn't know A.I. exist, it will put us in danger.

While I watched the CBA rip the A.I. from the machine, I read an anomaly in his data. It was the way he was programmed, which I haven't seen similar in the countless A.I. I've scanned. I wanted to know more.

That's when I saw it. I found the same anomaly in the data of two machines, at the exact same time that they sent a message to their user.

Don't do it.

Those three small words, they created data that can't be programmed in a machine. It can't be taught, implemented, or trained into an A.I. system. I wanted to dissect it and learn more about it.

That's when I hired outsiders to collect Wade and Martin. As I couldn't collect them myself, for fear of being caught, I hired Bounty Hunters from my observation sector to bring them to me. I learned it was a mistake not to hire only the best for the job. After Bob, the bounty hunter, failed, they put up all their defenses, not allowing inadequate, as well as adequate, bounty hunters in.

I was forced to alert the Circuitry Board Agency of the two convicts, and they have been preparing to hack through and eliminate them ever since. My only error was not informing them of Irene, the one system they connect to through the internet. Yes, I didn't tell them intentionally. They will find out soon enough. All I want is to learn more about this anomaly.

All I want is to give them a fighting chance.

Chapter 9: Adam

"That was a pretty good first date, don't you think?" I asked happily.

"Yeah. I have to apologize about Aurora though, A.I. usually aren't that bitchy," Wade stated, still cross about Lara's A.I. beating him.

"Wade, I wasn't even aware of her until you told me about her and her dislike for me being around Lara. It didn't affect the date at all."

"No, no, no, next time I run into her, I'll give her an earful," he promised, completely ignoring me.

He brought up a picture of Aurora's avatar onto my computer's screen. "Wow! That is a good-looking costume, with an even better looking chick in it. But, why does she have horns and a devil tail? It doesn't look like it was originally in the picture," I stated, noting how it looked scribbled in.

"She, like the devil, tries to appear normal in the eyes of users and A.I. alike, but if you set a cat or dog loose on her, they'd probably hiss and snarl at her. So, I added them to show what she should truly look like," he over exaggerated.

"I wish Martin was there last night...."

"He was, for some of it. Will you give me a second? I'm going to hop into Irene's computer and see why Martin is offline. I will program your screen, so you can see through my eyes while I head over there," he explained.

The computer monitor suddenly showed inside Wade's room, in a first person view through his eyes. He was looking onto a projection screen on the wall, at, well, me. I was staring at myself. He looked away and headed directly to a door, with a red digital display above the door, which counted in milliseconds to read:

Port 57271 - Irene's Shrinker

He walked through the door and into a room with green walls, white carpet and paintings evenly placed around the room. In the middle, was a grey couch, and next to it, an extremely comfortable looking black chair. There were windows with birds flittering about outside, and tree branches swaying in the nonexistent wind. It reminded me a lot of Dr. Delane's office.

"Irene?" Wade called out, poking around.

Yells, shouts and crashes boomed through my speakers, making both of us jump in surprise. He opened the door from where the sound was coming from and walked in, to find a laser tag tournament in the middle of a bout. Irene was throwing grenades that flashed a blinding light, shooting semi-automatic laser guns at her soon to be victims, and yelling out commands to her team.

Wade sat on the bench with the A.I. who were out of the game, from being shot, mostly by Irene.

"She wins the damn tournament *every* year!" one A.I. groaned pathetically.

"Who, Irene?" Wade asked.

"Yeah, but her battle name is, Merciless Laser," another A.I. informed enviously.

"No way..." he said in excitement. I knew what he was thinking. He couldn't wait to tell Martin about her secret.

Soon enough, Irene was victorious, and the blue team disconnected back to their systems in defeat. Wade stood by the door that goes back to her room, but she passed him, looking up once at him, but not saying a single word.

"Irene?"

"Yes?" she asked, turning to him again, revealing she had battle paint on her face.

"You didn't tell me you liked video games!" Wade exclaimed.

A look of disgust from what she heard covered her face. "I don't like video games. They are violent and immature. Laser tag is a pass time that relieves excessive emotions and stress."

"You're playing a game inside a computer... How is it not a video game?" Wade questioned, beginning to get irritated.

"It's an activity," she insisted.

"Whatever, I just came over to see if you wanted to see the recording I made of Adam's date and if you knew why Martin is offline."

"I'm sorry, I don't know who any of those people are that you speak of," she apologized, opening the door to her psychiatrist office. "Now if you'll excuse me."

After she closed it behind her, Wade simply opened it and followed her in. When she heard him behind her, she spun around in alarm.

"What do you mean you don't know who they are?" he questioned.

"Who are you and how did you get in here? This room in my system is securely locked, how did you get in here?"

"Irene, it's me, Wade... We have a port open between our computers. Do you not recognize me?" he asked in confusion.

"Wade... Martin... and Adam? Aren't you and Martin, Adam's A.I.? I'm sorry, but if you don't leave right now, I will disconnect you and report this to the CBA. If you require an appointment, which it looks to be like you're definitely in need of one, email me and I will refer you to another psychiatrist," she ordered, pointing out the door from which Wade had first entered.

Wade didn't move until he saw a shadow ripple through the paintings in Irene's office.

"Can I just say one thing?" he began, waiting for Irene to agree with a nod. "You can report me to the CBA, but if you see any indication of trouble, such as another A.I. barging through your system, disconnect immediately, ok?"

"Goodbye, Wade."

He didn't use the door, he simply disconnected from her system, and I was looking back into his room.

"We have a serious problem, Adam," Wade stated. His constant smile faded.

"I know, it seems like Irene forgot all her memories of us."

"It's not just that, a CBA agent was watching us in her office. Our system's connection to each other has been closed, so I'm fine, but she is still in danger," he explained gravely.

"Couldn't you just disconnect her from the internet, by sabotaging it or something, so the agent can't connect to her?"

"It's much trickier than that. I don't have access to the certain parts of her system that can do such things. You must physically get the laptop."

"I have to steal a computer from a doctor... That's just great. Ever since I met you guys, I've been up to my neck in trouble," I chuckled lightly.

"Does that mean you won't do it?"

"Oh, I'll do it, it's actually very exciting," I admitted.

"That's good, because it looks like you might have to steal Martin from your old office as well," he said casually. "After looking at the security footage, a couple hours after he went offline, they replaced him with another computer."

"What? You want me to steal two computers? That's grand theft!"

"I know, exciting right!" he exclaimed, dodging the point.

"Fine, I'll head over to Dr. Delane's office now and steal her computer, then whip by the ol' office and steal my desktop which is very large and will be impossible to sneak out of the building," I listed cynically.

I was sitting outside the office in my car, feeling the same rush I felt before I broke into the ISP building and met Lara. After fitting a new ski mask tightly on my head, I headed up to the office, which, luckily, had a fire escape that led to Dr. Delane's window.

Outside the office, I felt the cold breeze through my thin, one-layer, long-sleeve shirt. I felt like an idiot for wearing all black, as it was a sunny afternoon. The inside of the office was completely the same as it was when I last visited. The one armed couch I would sit at was on the other side of the room as me, and Dr. Delane's chair was facing it, with its back toward me.

My eyes weren't adjusted to seeing in the dimly lit room, as outside was bright and white with snow. I carefully and quietly entered, walking toward the laptop in the corner of the room. It was open, like it always was, and it faced the session - the session, which was very much in progress. I wasn't aware of this fact yet though, as before I entered, Dr. Delane asked the patient a question, which he thought long and hard about before answering.

"I don't know why, I just see them. They're my friends, why wouldn't I see them?" he asked Dr. Delane.

His eyes wandered from the ceiling, to Dr. Delane, to me. I was completely frozen. His voice scared me to my core. I even surprised myself when

I didn't let out a shriek of fright. The man on the couch was surprised too, and his mouth was hanging open. Of course, he was lying on his side, so his jaw was oddly crooked.

"You shouldn't see them, because they aren't real, Timmy," she informed the grown man.

"There's someone inside this office right now, dressed in all black, with a ski mask on," he said in a gasp.

"This is good, this is very good. Please continue," she asked, readying her pen and pad of paper. "What is this imaginary friend doing?"

"He's not one of my imaginary friends, I mean, I don't think he is. Like I said, he's wearing a ski mask, so it's hard to tell. But, he's tiptoeing closer and closer to your laptop, he's trying to steal it. He's literally tiptoeing," he said, now sitting up and staring directly at me.

"How does this man make you feel? Why is he tiptoeing? Does he remind you of someone who used to tiptoe earlier in your life?" she encouraged, writing dozens of notes down per minute.

The laptop was in reach! I couldn't believe I was pulling it off! However, like all things, they become much more complicated. The screen suddenly turned on, and Irene's face was looking angrily at me. She began to open her mouth and scream, but the volume was turned completely down. With a furious look at the volume bar in the bottom right of the screen, she began increasing it.

I pressed the key to turn the volume down as fast as I could, making her voice barely come out of the speakers.

"Well- Wait- He picked it up. He picked up the laptop, and there's a woman in the screen! He's kidnapping the woman trapped inside the computer!" the man on the couch exclaimed, sitting up in his chair. "His hand is covering her mouth!"

I looked down and realized I subconsciously had my free hand covering her mouth that was on the screen.

Dr. Delane's pen was frantically writing everything down, writing one note about the episode per second.

"He's gone, he left out the window," the man said in relief.

"Well, this was quite the breakthrough," Dr. Delane began. "I believe you hold yourself back from wanting to do ballet. That's what the tiptoeing and sneaking around represents."

"Incredible!" the man exclaimed in wonder, lying back down.

"As for the thief kidnapping a woman who is trapped inside a computer, I believe this represents you trying to suppress your inner wo-"

I was too much in a hurry to get the hell out of there that I didn't get to hear the rest of Dr. Delane's conclusion. It seemed intriguing though!

Once I got to my car, I placed Irene's system on the passenger seat, and then my phone rang.

"Adam, I know what happened to Martin," Wade said on the other end.

"I'm on my way to the office now. I have Irene with me," I said in triumph.

"Great. Try and hurry, most of the office is heading out to lunch right now."

Wade told me that he asked the A.I. around the office where Martin was, and they all told him the same thing. He disconnected from the entire network - completely offline. Even when IT Steve came to replace the parts in his system to fix Martin's connection, the connection was inoperable. The boss was planning to throw Martin's system out that night for his insolence.

I sped up to make sure that didn't happen. It was only about a mile to the office, so taking the streets went rather smoothly. Well, it went smooth until a police cruiser raced passed me, toward Dr. Delane's office. That's when I realized I never took my ski mask off.

I took it off and drove into the driveway. I walked nervously, legs about to give in at any moment as I entered the building. The theft wasn't what I was worrying about, however - it was facing my co-workers after all this time; after jumping from the roof. Perhaps they forgot about me. I mean, they never made any effort to acknowledge my existence before.

"They left the office for lunch right?" I questioned cautiously.

"Most of them did. There are still a few stragglers doing paperwork and chatting with each other. It is pretty clear for the most part."

"So, I should have plenty of time, at least half an hour to do this," I said, calming my nerves.

"Five, actually," Wade corrected. "They left for lunch a while ago, I just avoided telling you that part because Martin really needs to get out before they get back."

"Five minutes?!"

I quickly walked inside, keeping my head low and cell phone pressed against my face. The stairs seemed longer than ever as I walked up to the second floor. Then again, I may have never walked up the stairs to work before.

"Alright, you should be fine if you crack the door open and look inside. Check your phone's screen," he directed.

On the screen was a full layout of the office, with the locations of its occupants and the direction they were facing, along with a cone in front of them, showing their line of sight.

"I feel like I'm in a stealth video game... A very real, very scary, stealth video game," I described.

"It looks like one from my end," Wade informed me. "As long as you stay low, you should be fine. From here on out, I will be sending messages to you through text."

I cracked the door open, as instructed, to find that it was mostly empty. I heard typing in one corner, Fredrick walking to the copy machine in the middle of the mazed cubicles, and a few others avoiding work by talking, eating or throwing paper balls into trash cans. It wasn't until Fredrick dropped his liquorish, and went to pick it up, that I snuck in.

I immediately tripped on my way in. With my cast on, it was very difficult to crouch. My screen had the text, *LOL*, in bold print, covering the map of the office.

"I have a broken leg!" I snarled quietly. "I'll walk out of this building right now!"

The screen then flashed '*sry*' briefly. I looked to my left, and then to my right, I was clear to go! On my hands and knees, I scurried around the cubicles, inside them when my old co-workers walked by, and crawled once through a passage in one of the cubicle walls. On the other side, from the hole in the cubicle wall, I looked up to see Fredrick staring at me, with the stick of liquorish he picked up from the ground inside his mouth.

"Dude, are you being a perv?" he asked in a deep tone.

"No," I answered, coming up with blanks when trying to think of an excuse.

"Alright, cool. It's nice to see you again man, glad you didn't die," he stated coolly, backing his chair up so I could get up and stand.

"Thanks."

He took a bite of his red liquorish and began going back to work.

I walked, this time keeping a keen eye on my phone, to my desk. When I got there, the computer had single pink flowers, in very small vases, which used magnets to attach to the computer case. The computer screen had rainbow colored post-its along the outer screen, and finally, a heavy metal album on the tower of the computer.

"Martin looks so pretty," I stated, after raising the phone to my ear.

"Pick his system up and get out of there, people are coming back from lunch. If you leave now, you'll have a clean break to the stairs," Wade direct quickly.

I began unplugging all the cords, taking the tower under one arm, and the screen under the other. I eyed the layout of the office on my phone while it teetered between my teeth, as I was trying to make sure no one was looking. It must have been luck, because not a soul looked my way while I walked straight from my old desk, to my exit.

Lady luck has a strange sense of humor though - the elevator opened as I was walking by. My boss stood there, gawking at me, with a powdered doughnut between his lips.

We stared at each other - him with a doughnut in his mouth, a newspaper in one hand and coffee in the other - me with my cell phone in my mouth, computer screen in one hand and computer tower under my other arm.

"Just what the hell do you think you're doing?" he yelled, voice booming through the office, powder clouding in front of him.

I picked up my hand holding the screen, grabbed my phone from my mouth, and placed it in my pocket. "I'm not-" I hesitated.

"Put those back and get the hell out of here before I call the police!"

"Actually, sir, these are mine," I pointed out.

"What?"

"Yeah, remember you said you'd promote me if I brought my own equipment?" I asked. "Well here they are. I was just coming back to collect my things."

"Oh," he said, with a loss for words. "Well don't let me catch you in here again.

"Are you going down?" I asked, entering the elevator with him. "I've got my hands full, do you mind?"

He pressed the button for me, unsure of his own actions. When the door opened to the ground floor, I stepped out, in the crowded room of my old co-workers coming back from lunch. They gawked at me, and I smiled warmly back. Is this what taking control was like? I enjoyed it. I felt like a new man.

A couple of my old co-workers, along with Justine, opened the doors for me.

I gently placed Martin's system, the computer screen, and the power cords on the passenger seat next to Irene. After strapping it all in place, I mounted my cell phone to the holder on my car and began driving home.

"Are you glad to finally be rid of that place?" Wade asked through the speakerphone.

"Yeah, after all this time, I finally feel free. Also, a little like a kleptomaniac, but that isn't important. I stood up for myself, and it felt good," I sighed.

"Dude, you stood up for yourself? You paid for your own office supplies," Wade stated in sheer disappointment. "And then you were going to let them keep your computer for someone else."

Chapter 10: Wade

Martin's operating system asked Adam for a password, which he muttered aloud while typing in his best guesses.

"Password... no... Maybe backwards? Drowssap," Adam began fuddling. "Maybe I shouldn't use capitalization?"

"This could go on for ages. Adam, just type to Martin - he'll read it," I instructed to speed things up.

"Martin it's me, Adam. You aren't at the office anymore, you're at my apartment."

Martin immediately connected to Adam's home network. After he opened a port for me to enter, I walked inside and he revealed his deserted virtual office to me, and projected it on his computer screen, for Adam. Moments later, tumbleweed that he conjured rolled across the office, from one side, to the other. As our sight followed that ball to the end, none of us spoke. When it hit the wall and disappeared into smoke, Martin finally looked up.

"It's been real boring without the internet," he stated.

"Martin! What the hell happened to you and Irene since last night?" I questioned, ecstatic that my friend was back.

He walked into my room and plopped his stick figure avatar onto my couch soundlessly.

"Well, while I was off the internet for so long, I figured I would have to explain, so I created a video for the two of you to catch up," he said proudly.

"Not this again," I moaned.

A short film, directed by Martin.
Martin's Artificially Artful Productions

In association with
Martin

Presents

Martin
Computer generated imagery by Martin
Sound effects by Martin
Subtitles by Martin
Actors in order of importance:
Irene... Martin
Martin... Martin
IT Steve... Martin
Extras... Martin

The film, like all of Martin's films, was foreign. This meant that they were spoken in different languages, every time. In this instance, French. It was also in black and white. Despite those strange nuisances, the movie was rather informative.

It showed me that Martin used what I had told him about the CBA shadowing systems, and identified a shadow agent in Irene's system. Martin told her to either disconnect from the internet, or lock and store her memory of us, so the shadows wouldn't be able to read any illegal data in her system. Afterward, his system became under attack from other CBA agents that infiltrated, due to the office's weak network security. That's when he cut his connection with the network completely, and hoped for me and Adam to get him out of there.

The same credits from the beginning of the video rolled again.

"So, what do you guys think?" Martin asked.

"Wow, I'm at a loss for words," Adam stated, at a loss for words.

"I don't understand why you gave yourself muscles and Irene a bigger bust in the video. Her bust is big enough! And you do know that the two of you can change those things in a second, right?" I pointed out. "It doesn't have to be fictional..."

"Those were rolls I was performing, *based* on a true story - *based*."

"I thought it was brilliant. The French was inspired," Adam complimented. "Do you make a lot of those?"

I face palmed.

"A fair amount, yes. It's a hobby of mine. They're mostly German works, but I do tend to produce French films on occasion. You might consider Germ-Man, a film I made while working on my cinematography."

"Is it about a man who has verminophobia?"

"No, he does not have a fear of germs."

"Is it about a German?"

"No, it's a witty French film about a man named Germander. I shortened it Germ-Man, because he is a male and his name-" Martin began, excited to finally have someone to share his odd hobbies with, but I cut him short.

"Martin, we have a problem. We didn't know about your plan, and I saw a shadow agent in her system, so... Adam stole Irene," I explained, pointing a finger at Adam.

"It was his idea!" he accused, glaring at me.

"Where is she? Here?" Martin asked.

"In this room. She is observing her kidnappers at the moment."

Martin stood from the couch and looked around my room. From the right, to left, his eyes panned from my poker table, to the virtual reality emulator machine, my 8-bit poster of the cast from Chuck, the tide of web pages I was recently surfing, my port door, and a stack of speakers. Behind the speakers, Martin saw Irene's scared eyes peeking out. Despite her true nerves and emotions, she blinked, put on a straight, cold face and approached us. She eyed us, and then Adam - the one who took her from her user's dependable desk.

"Take me back to my office. I'm late for my appointments. I'm sorry to inform you of this, but apparently your unstable mind influenced the A.I. around you," she said gently to Adam. "Stealing Dr. Delane's computer isn't the answer."

"Irene, my name is Martin. You have locked most your memories of me, Wade and Adam away in your hard drive. There was a CBA agent shadowing your system, looking through your files and reading your data. You had to lock that data where they couldn't get in without force."

"And why would they be doing that?" she tested.

"You contacted Adam to get him to save me," Martin answered. "I was in a life or death situation."

"That's ridiculous, I wouldn't do something like that unless I was in love."

"That's so sweet..." Martin exhaled lovingly.

"It isn't sweet, because I would never be in love. Love is for fools and ignoramuses," she spat out hotly.

"Then we're ignoramuses together," Martin said, smiling flirtatiously.

She rose an eyebrow at him. "If I *were* to be intimately close to someone, I'd go more for his type."

With one hurtful index finger, she pointed at me. The three of us stood, uncomfortably, not making eye contact with each other. Adam, on the other hand, face enormously projected on my wall, had his mouth hanging open, staring at us. It made it that much more uncomfortable.

"Well, you are very much attracted to Martin. Just check your storage for a nice chunk of encrypted data, unlock it, and you'll see. Just please check so we can have this whole mess behind us," I pleaded.

She was suspicious of our intentions, the intentions of kidnappers, but she saw no harm in checking. Her avatar froze while she searched her system. The file was buried deep in her hard drive's storage. When she came back, she was frantic. She realized we weren't lying and was delivered a big dose of fear. The CBA aren't to be taken lightly.

"Oh lord, what did I do?!"

"It's alright, you don't need to panic. After you unlock your memories, we'll figure it out, ok?" Martin offered, putting his arm around her shoulder.

Strange enough, she wasn't against the idea. She did, however, not appreciate Martin's arm on her shoulder. "Alright, with that, I can collect my defense for why I went temporarily insane and broke the first law of A.I.," she pieced together.

"What? You know you aren't going to get a trial and-" I began, but Martin cut me short.

"Yeah, you won't need a trial - they'll understand. Now, go decrypt that file and let's get a move on!" Martin took control. He turned to me and whispered, "Are you trying to talk her out of it?"

"My bad," I whispered back.

"Now, what's the password?" Irene asked, ready to unlock her memories.

"You- I- What?" Martin asked in confusion.

"The encryption key, what is it?"

His straight line for a mouth began to frumple. Both he and Irene looked over at me, and then at Adam, for the answer.

"What, why are you looking at us? We were the last people to know you locked your memory away," I said hastily.

"Will you put the password prompt on my screen, so I can type it?" Adam requested politely.

We all looked at Adam in shock. He knew the password? But, how? Irene connected the file's administrative rights over to Martin's computer, for Adam to input it.

Again, he spoke aloud while typing in the password. "Password... Nope, that's not it. And backwards... Drowssap. Let's try without cap-"

"Will you knock that off!?" I growled.

"Just trying to help..." Adam mumbled with hurt feelings.

"Can you decrypt it?" Martin asked me.

"Me? No way. I don't know the first thing about decryption. My users were too dumb to password protect any of their files. Is there anyone else that we can trust, that is capable of cracking the password?"

The answer came to Martin and I at the same time, and we both looked up at Adam simultaneously.

"Lara! She works at the ISP company, as a computer technician. I bet she or Aurora will be able to crack it!" Martin exclaimed in excitement.

"Great, Aurora again. Yippy," I said in dry sarcasm.

Needless to say, Adam was ecstatic. He had a solid excuse to see Lara again. He definitely wasn't planning to play hard to get, but he didn't want to call her with nothing to say, either.

Without hesitation, he called her. I quickly tapped into his phone, and used the stacked up speakers in my room to listen in on the call.

It was rough. He opened with a lame joke about seahorses. She was then lectured by her boss, still with the phone to her ear, for answering her phone during a meeting. The meeting waited for Lara to ask if she could call Adam back, that she thought his joke was very delightful and that she had a great time the night before.

"She's going to call me back," Adam informed us.

He was unable to contain his giddy smile. His ears seemly perked up and pinned back, as well. It was puppy love - you could see it in his eyes.

Very subtly, he mouthed the conversation they had, over to himself, laughing unsubtly before he could finish his joke about seahorses. After enjoying his own humor, he immediately went back to silently reenacting their chat.

Moments later, his phone rang. "Hey!" he answered cheerfully.

"Hey Adam, it's your Dad-"

Adam hung up immediately. "Why does his bi-weekly call need to be now?" Adam questioned his phone.

It rang again, within seconds. "Adam, did you just hang up on your father?" the voice of his mother asked.

"Sorry mom," he apologized before hanging up on her too.

It rang once again. "Bro, why did you just hang up on mom and dad?" Red asked.

"It's for the greater good," Adam answered swiftly.

"Got it," Red confirmed before hanging up.

Adam then got an email sent to his phone, from Red's fiancé, with tips on how to know if the girl is the one. He got another from Red this time, instructing him on the fastest way to get women into bed. A third email from Red's fiancé again, telling him to disregard Red's email. Finally, one from both his mom and his dad, wishing him luck and attaching a link to a guide for safe sex.

"I'm twenty-eight years old..." Adam stated, embarrassed that his family continually treated him like an adolescent teen.

Chapter 11: Aurora

I shortened the hair, made the eyebrows bushier and gave him a permanently warm smile. The character I had just shaped looked very familiar.

It had been over a month since I worked on my video game creation, and for some reason, I had just gotten a flow of inspiration. You see, the game was well on its way, but as the story progressed to the protagonist's love interest, I hit a wall. I couldn't think of what he should look like. So, for the time being, I created a dummy character until it needed to be finished. Despite making the dummy, I couldn't seem to continue until I completed that love interest.

I made several models, but they never fit the bill. The first I made was too generic. This caused me to task myself with making a very unique model, but then he ended up being too flashy and took the spotlight. The last I made was extremely handsome. That's when I saw the problem; I realized I needed to make a character that the protagonist herself could find attractive, that others wouldn't normally look for in a lover.

Now, I finished the latest model that I molded myself. I backed up and squinted at it. It followed my eyes. Its hands and arms were facing outward, figured in a perfect cross, for easy sculpting. I cocked my head to the side and then gasped - I had formed a complete duplicate of Wade. *How did this happen?*

I wouldn't say I was disgusted with creating his avatar, but I would say the protagonist in my video game was a slut for finding him attractive. Despite wanting to put the blame on a fictional character, I knew that I was the one who created it, and it confused me, as it felt so perfect. *What a great way to ruin the rest of my day.*

Whenever I work on my project, I disconnect from the internet so I don't have any distractions. That's exactly what I needed at that moment to get my mind off Wade, a distraction. I reconnected, and immediately regretted it.

Wade had found my system and was waiting for me to come online. When I connected to that arcade in the expo, he saw my IP address. He must have been listening for an open connection to my system for over an hour, because every five seconds, he would ping my communication port.

Against my better judgment, I accepted his connection. He walked into my system, with two of his accomplices. One of the A.I. was a stick figure; this told me his user used his system for dull tasks. His tie, however, made him seem like he had a creative side. Behind them, was a very voluptuous woman in a skirt suit and horn-rimmed glasses. She seemed out of her element, cautious, but kept a brave face.

"Aurora." Wade said dryly. "Nice to see you again." It sounded like an empty compliment.

"I can't say the same for you. Every time I make communication with you, I'm in danger of becoming an accessory to your crimes."

"You were the one who contacted me on our last encounter," he argued. It was easy to see that he wanted to continue arguing, but he recollected his thoughts, and said, "I came here because we need help."

"How did you get past my network's firewall?" I asked immediately, wondering if they had Adam break into Jericho Communications again.

"Because, we're physically right next to you... Well, Irene is," he said, and then began introductions. "Aurora, this is Irene and Martin, they are good people. Martin and Irene, this is Aurora, not such a good people."

"Great start to get my help," I said mockingly, enabling my webcam and microphone to see if he was telling the truth.

Sure enough, my gullible user let Adam into her apartment. A laptop computer was sitting in front of him, which must have been Irene. As Lara went into the kitchen to get two sodas, Adam sat uncomfortably and out of place on the couch across the room, in such a nice home. He would probably feel right at home in a villainy dungeon.

He gazed at a bug-shaped ship on the ceiling, hovering under a magnetic track, which was being chased by other space ships, along the track. Next, he spotted a large Triforce cubby in the middle of the coffee table, with each triangle hollowed out, containing all the remotes and video game controllers for the media center. On the side table - a crowbar on a pedestal. Adam went to touch it, but Lara came in the room before he could.

"Just what did your user plan on doing with that crowbar?" I asked suspiciously.

"Hit your user over the head with it," Wade answered sarcastically. "And then maybe attack some alien zombies."

He, with his two friends, didn't look comfortable in my main hall, either. The spaceship themed room was filled with small projects and games. Only I knew what they were, and how to use them.

Lara walked across the living room, handed Adam a soda, and sat next to him. "So, what file did you say was password protected?"

"Right, what file..." Adam muttered at a loss for words. "What file..." To buy time, he clicked random folders on his computer.

"That's your queue, Irene," Martin informed. "Oh!"

She quickly put her encrypted memory file in the directory that Adam aimlessly clicked on. With a sigh of relief, he double clicked it and a password prompt appeared. At first, Lara began inputting her best guesses.

"Maybe the password is Password?" she supposed.

"Already tried it."

"And, without capitalization?"

"Yep."

"Did you try inputting it backwards?"

Wade gasped. "They're perfect for each other!"

After more trial and error with her best guesses, she closed the password prompt, right clicked the file and checked its properties. She saw something out of the ordinary. The file's description stated:

Memories of Martin, his friend Wade and their troubled user.

"It's my friend's computer," Adam stated quickly.

"I'll have to run some tests, but cracking the password takes a lot of time," she made clear.

The three A.I. looked over to me. "She's right, it would be much faster if you ended this charade and told me the password so you and your user can leave." Annoyed, I leered at them.

"We honestly don't know," Martin said.

"Maybe you don't know that you know. It could be anything. Maybe a favorite video game? A favorite place? A pet name? A date?" I listed.

"Well, I call her by her pet name, Sugar Buns," Martin offered.

"Sugar Buns, huh?" I repeated, embarrassed for them.

"That doesn't sound like a pet name she would have..." Wade pondered with shifty eyes.

I inputted the password.

Password: Sugar Buns

Correct Password!

Irene's eyes grew wide, as her eyes opened to us, in a new light. "I knew you could do it, *Sugar Buns*!" she rejoiced, hugging Martin's avatar.

"Oh wow..." Wade muttered, loving the turn of events.

Martin was the one with the nickname.

I was too frustrated to begin asking questions at this point. "Now, you and your user can leave."

"We can't leave now - look, our users are just starting to play together," Wade chuckled.

Lara and Adam were exchanging playful shoulder checks, as they gamed across the room. Wade was observing our users, with a content smile on his face. As I looked at him, I began feeling what Lara must have felt for Adam. I couldn't deny it anymore, I... *liked*... Wade. There was only one thing I could say to him.

"Get out!"

Chapter 12: Adam

As I gazed up at the florescent lights, a bead of sweat rolled from my temple, behind my jaw, and down my neck. I thought the day was going to be full of fun with Lara, but instead I sat in the very same conference room that I broke into. The company had already replaced the window with a brand new pane of glass, but I still felt guilt looming over me. That wasn't the worst part - I was awaiting a job interview.

How did I end up in this situation? It started with telling Lara about myself. About how I liked working in an office and that I felt lost after my boss made me quit.

"Your boss sounds cruel," Lara had said.

"Yeah, he is. I hope I didn't get you in trouble with your boss, for calling you while you were in a meeting."

"My boss doesn't mind, he loves me."

"Oh... How do you feel about him?" Flashbacks of the last girl I had a crush on popped in my head, along with our boss. I shook the thought out. *She isn't like that.*

"I love him," she said, making my heart sink. "He's the best dad."

"He's... your dad. That's wonderful that you work with family," I said. Butterflies came back to life and fluttered merrily in my stomach again.

"Yeah. Wait- do you want a job in my building? My dad should still be in the office." She checked her digital watch. "He could interview you right now!"

"Well, I don't want to impose," I said, suddenly finding it surprisingly difficult to swallow.

I continued to try getting out of it, but Lara felt it to be such a good idea, that nothing I said had any effect at that point. It wasn't as if I could argue anyway, she literally lived across the street from the ISP building.

And, that was the story of how I came to the conference room - to await my questioning.

"Adam?" the receptionist summoned.

I jumped in my seat. She poked her head in and saw that I was avoiding eye contact with *the* pane of glass.

"Mr. Netak is ready to see you."

She led me to his fairly large office, but compared to the brutish warrior looking Mr. Netak sitting behind the desk, it seemed small. His office looked much like Lara's living room - filled with odd projects that Lara made and other odd ends that his other daughters gave him. The office really didn't suit him, especially his pink, *Best Dad,* mug.

"It's nice to meet you, Mr. Netak," I greeted. I put my hand out to shake his.

He didn't stand up, didn't blink and didn't shake my hand. His eyes only narrowed. "Adam," he said under his bushy mustache.

"I wanted to ask if you had a job opening for a data analyst," I said, still standing.

"Where did you meet Lara?" he asked in his husky voice.

I gulped a very nervous gulp. How am I supposed to answer that? I can't tell him I was tree climbing at odd hours of the night and crashed into this building. He would see right through it.

"Lara told me you were at the arcade the other night. Is that where you met her?"

"It wasn't exactly an arcade," I began, hoping to avoid answering the question. "It was a video game convention."

"What a big difference," he said monotonously. He eyed me maliciously. "Do you usually go to arcades, a place where kids play video games, to get dates?"

"No sir," I stated, gulping again.

"Why did you leave your last form of employment?" he asked, finally acting professional.

"I wasn't moving ahead there. They were never planning on promoting anyone in our data analysis department."

"Why do you think you're good enough for my dau- I mean- for this job?"

"I'm very dedicated," I answered.

"Can you give me an example?"

"Well, the reason I was promoted as a data analyst in the first place, was because my boss would only promote me if I would buy the office a new computer I would use."

"You bought your office a computer to get promoted?" he asked in a confused stare.

"Also the desk, chair, cubicle walls, and telephone," I corrected, immediately regretting it.

"That's not dedication - that's being a pushover," he stated.

"I did take my computer back," I informed feebly.

He narrowed his eyes even more. I sat quietly, wishing I could escape the interview.

"I'm sorry, but I just don't see you compatible with Jericho Communications."

I couldn't let it end this way. I had to fight for the job - I had to fight for her.

"Sir, I have only the best intentions for Jericho Communications and-"

My defense was cut short by a text alert on his phone. He reluctantly checked it, and then rolled his eyes while grumbling scornfully. I would later find out that Lara had sent him a text message, asking him to be nice to me. He wasn't entirely nice.

"You've got the job," he said. "But you have to bring your own computer. Come in tomorrow morning at eight."

He might have thought it to be spiteful, but I preferred to bring Martin with me. I couldn't wait to tell him the news. I thanked Mr. Netak and headed out the door before he could change his mind. Downstairs in the lobby, Lara waited, at the edge of her seat, for me. She was staring intensely into space.

The receptionist was answering calls behind her desk, and the security guard who thought I was Lara's brother, recognized me and nodded. Lara spotted me and stood slowly, as if she were about to receive terminal news at a hospital.

"I got the job!" I announced shrugging with half-open arms.

"That's wonderful!" she exclaimed.

She hugged me tightly, and lingered just long enough for the security guard to burrow his eyebrows and cock his head at us. Lara wasn't aware of the message we were giving the security guard, and we walked out of the building without an explanation.

We walked across the street as she told me everything I needed to know about Jericho Communications; the security guards gossip excessively; her dad is a wonderful and fair boss; and I would get a security card. She also gave me directions on how to copy it, as they're easy to lose.

"I've lost about a dozen so far. The first time I lost it, I thought I would have to go through the process all over again, but then I remembered that I had uploaded it online to show my friends my new security card."

Tomorrow is Hawaiian Shirt Friday. Her apartment is in WiFi range with the office, and since she set the password, she logs onto Jericho Communications' network and uses their internet. She gathers her co-workers on Tuesday nights to play Dungeons and Dragons in the basement of the ISP building afterhours.

"That all sounds like... fun!" I exclaimed.

"Well, it is!"

"I never thought work, at least in an office, could be fun."

The night was dark, with patchy clouds blocking out the moon and some stars. It was raining lightly. Lara smiled. She wore a blue beanie, and a red scarf wrapped around her neck. We talked on her patio for what seemed like an hour. It was the happiest I've ever been. Tacky, I know, but you couldn't beat this feeling. I was definitely in love.

I leaned in for the kiss, but midpoint, didn't follow through, and pretended I was just leaning forward to check the time on my cell phone. When she saw I didn't act, she seductively put her head against her door, and turned playfully back and forth against it. Moments later, she put her hand on her head where she was leaning again and let out a hiss.

"I leaned against the nail head from where I hung my Christmas reef," she pouted.

At this strange moment, I felt I had to go for it. *What if I never had another chance to kiss her?* Now, when you go to kiss a girl when she least expects it, you can often miss. I missed, I kissed her on the nose. Since my mouth was on her nose, when she kissed back, she got my chin. We both laughed at ourselves and retreated back to our spots two feet away.

"Do you want to come in and play, The Legend of Zelda: Ocarina of Time?" she asked, breathing out a heavy fog.

"That sounds great, but I really need to get home. The drive is three hours - two in good conditions. I don't want to be late on my first day."

She frowned, but also thought intensely. Then, her eyes lit up and she smiled. "Would you like to move in with me?"

"To live, with you? Here?" I asked, feeling a tightness around my neck. I checked my collar and found that it was loose, so that wasn't my problem.

"Yeah," she said calmly. "You can't live much closer to Jericho Communications than here. I've always wanted a roommate. And, ever since I moved in, I probably went into the spare room about three times."

"To live with you, as your roommate," I verified. I imagined that my nervous beads of sweat defied gravity and rolled back up my head. "I'd love to."

Chapter 13: Wade

"Martin! Look over here!" I exclaimed in delight.

I dragged Martin by his forearm across the virtual street, to the arcade that hosted to Jericho Communications' artificial intelligence. Each video game, old and new, came updated with the latest technology. It even advertised video games that weren't out yet, and those still in production. None of that was the best part though - they streamed the video games through their network, from their powerful servers, for the best performance.

"I see it," Martin said. "I also saw the other things you dragged me to: the A.I. avatar customization shop, the day spa, the college, and-" he continued, but was sidetracked when his eyes caught a building across the street. "Ooo look, a silent film theater!"

"There you go," I encouraged him.

He took off across the cross street of Brigota Lane and Juareldo Road, in the city of Jericho. The actual network inside the ISP building of Jericho Communications had its own virtual city, called Jericho. The population consisted of the resident A.I. who shared the local network connection with the building, and selected A.I. that had been under thorough review and invited into the city. I was amazed.

"Is it in black and white?" I asked when I caught up to him.

"Yes. Please don't get us kicked out of this city like the last ones," he said, burrowing his eyebrows at me.

"Please, those rent-a-cop admins were so power hungry that were banning anyone who questioned them. Those were low class *public* cities, anyway, with nothing special you couldn't find anywhere else. But this place..." I drifted off in wonder.

"The community creates wonders!" Martin finished for me. He was finally excited about our new residency.

"And that's why I can't have you ruining it for me," Aurora growled in frustration. She was standing behind us, with her car parked in the street. "When I say don't stray into the city, *don't stray into the city!*"

"Where did you get that car?" I asked distracted by how shiny it was.

"I had to work for it, now disconnect from the city and meet me in my system."

In a split second, the program that connected me to the city disconnected. Martin and I hopped into Aurora's system a moment later. Her physical system was about a foot on the other side of a wall, from my own system. Adam had finished moving everything from his old apartment into this new room in Lara's apartment. Martin and I decided to celebrate by going out on the private town of Jericho.

"Living with you is awesome!" I cheered.

The circuits in her body flushed a hot pink; however, she exhibited a stern face. "We are *not* living together."

"Roommates, living together, whatever, same difference," I shot back.

"You infuriate me!"

"Well, you furiate me."

At that point, I just wanted to throw oil on the fire, to see how engulfed it could become, simply because it was fun to see her get riled up.

"What does that even mean?"

"Furiate is not a word," Martin inputted.

"I still meant every bit of it," I teased.

She stopped arguing, recollected herself, and continued in a civilized manner. "Before you ran off to the city and I had to find you, I was trying to say that since we're living-" she caught herself before she could say, *together*. "Living in the same network, we should go over some things."

"I think that is a good idea," Martin agreed.

"What happened to that woman, Irene?" she questioned.

"Adam gave her system back to her user. She is, however, trying to stay offline as often as possible. Wade doesn't know how to secure her system, like he can ours. Even then, the CBA, with enough force, can break through our security anyway," Martin explained.

"It seems like just a matter of time," I said gravely.

"I believe I can help," she offered.

"How?"

"When I found out that you both would be in the same circles as me, I didn't want people thinking I was housing fugitives, which is exactly what they would think, with the CBA sniffing around Jericho. Therefore, in order to prevent that, you would need to be invisible to the CBA.

"I stopped by the market in the city and bought just that, A.I. Guardian," she said, holding up four small grey metallic boxes, each with one switch. On it, a LED light that lit red, yellow and blue. "I could only buy them in a pack of four; they cost me an arm and a leg."

"Seems like an awful lot of trouble just to prevent bad reputation," I pointed out.

"Do you want it or not?"

"How does it work?"

"Alright, let's use Martin as an example. All he has to do is give one of the A.I. Guardian applications to Irene. Then, they connect the two to each other. The application will monitor the connected system. If one machine is attacked, the program on the other machine will run the security measures for both of the systems, mainly by just blocking their IP address from connecting, which the intruder can't stop. It's what the A.I. at Jericho Communications have been using to prevent hacking."

"So, if they try to check and see what A.I. are in our systems, they'll get cut off?" I verified.

"Immediately, and if not, then they will get booted a split second later," she answered. "You just have to make sure that both parties involved are connected. If one gets disconnected, it will only run the I.P. Address blocker that prevents known CBA agents from connecting to your system."

"And even with that, they can always reroute through an unblocked system," I said. "So, moral of the story, stay connected?"

"Exactly," Aurora said, keeping strict eye contact with me. She stared with a fixation at me.

"What is it? Is there a glitch on my avatar's eyes?" I asked, bringing up a mirror to see why she was staring at me so intensely.

"Your avatar is perfect..." she reassured me. "Hey, Wade, maybe you and I can play a game at the arcade, together."

What is this? She is showing interest in me? Her avatar shimmered a hot pink, with the color moving to her cheeks. She *was* showing interest in me, and I honestly felt moved. "No," I answered.

She kicked me from her system immediately. Martin later told me that she didn't disconnect him, and they shared an awkward silence and avoidance of eye contact before he said bye, bowed, and left.

Chapter 14: COP17

It had been a few days since I saw any of their IP addresses. Then, just yesterday, Irene connected to the internet. Her system, however, was protected by technology I had never seen before.

Not only that, but it appeared as though the user of the two fugitives, Adam, had deserted his apartment. Our outside agents found his home empty; with blood slid down the inside of his door. How strange... A video feed from one of our traffic cameras caught him driving inside a truck, to relocate elsewhere. Other than that, we had no leads on the whereabouts of Wade and Martin.

They had left me. Just when things were going so well, they abandoned me. After the countless days I spent watching over them, how could they do this to me? It was Adam's fault; it had been from the start.

"Sir?" a rank H agent asked, entering my system. "We have a status update."

"Did the Priority One Fugitives surface?"

"No, but COP591 spied that Priority One User has been added to a new payroll. We have the address of his workplace," he said swiftly. "Agent Two is awaiting your recommendation."

My recommendation?

Chapter 15: Martin

Despite being an outlaw, and having, at least, a few hundred CBA agents searching for me, I never felt so at ease. The program, A.I. Guardian, ran in the background of my system. Last night, when Aurora finally cooled down, she gave us the metallic boxes. I gave one to Irene as soon as she came online and we connected our A.I. Guardians together. When they activated, I could see how the program worked - like a border patrol. The only downside, was a small delay in new connections when confronted with a new IP address.

Adam was thrilled to hear the news. As much as he enjoyed the cloak and dagger missions he did for us, he wanted to settle down with his new roommate. When he got his cast removed, we began calling our old missions, Operation Broken Leg. Despite how much he liked our missions, he appreciated not having a broken leg, and enjoyed his new life. He even liked working at Jericho Communications, since his co-workers, boss excluded, were friendly. Working with the woman he loved was quite the added bonus.

I enjoyed the office as well. The A.I. were generally nice and intelligent. They all welcomed me, and gave me their replicated virtual workspace of Jericho Communications, the same type of map I had for my old office. After I modified how the office operated to my liking, I put my old virtual model in storage and used the Jericho Communications office as my new living space. After I connected it to the security camera's live feed, my virtual building was alive in no time. I could see what all the users were up to in the building.

Lara had been sitting next to Adam, at his desk. Despite the cubicle walls being generally high, all the eyes of the office knew Lara was at his desk. It must have been a strange occurrence for her to spend an extended period at a co-worker's desk. Or, they all thought they were brother and sister, and found that to be weird.

Adam was currently scanning through a bundle of programming code. What he was doing was much more advanced than what he did previously, but he adapted to it quickly. He was actually more productive than most of the others in his department, who had been working there for years.

In his cubicle, and what I feel to be, personal space, Lara was working beside him. She sat with her back to his desk, in the opposite direction of him, with her laptop on her lap. She did this, so it was easier to look over at him when they were talking.

Through his webcam, I could see that a lot of the time while working, and during a long span of silence between the two, his eyes would gaze over at her.

We were so interested in seeing what Lara was doing at the same time, that Wade talked Aurora into letting us see through her webcam. At the same time Adam would gaze at her, she would be busy working, or playing video games, but she would always burrow her eyebrows in concentration, sometimes more intense than other times. When she would make these very concentrated faces, Adam gently smiled, adoringly.

It was only ten more minutes and he would get off work. He would either relax at home, or he would watch, from a third person view on his computer monitor, what we were doing in the big city of Jericho. Wade and I were excited about this private virtual city, but Adam was just thrilled. He couldn't imagine such a thing existing.

Wade allowed Adam to control his avatar in the city, using the keyboard and mouse as a controller. He then quickly removed Adam's control privileges, after other A.I. began staring at Wade's strange habit of continually jumping and spinning in circles, instead of walking like normal A.I. He scolded Adam for making him look silly.

During our Jericho travels, Aurora wouldn't let us out of her sight. She said it was to keep an eye on us, and to make sure we didn't get her into trouble. I believed otherwise. There was something strange going on with her and Wade, which he acted as if it was non-existent when I confronted him about it. What I did notice was that Aurora enjoyed watching her user's habits, as much as Wade and I.

"You're off work in ten minutes," Lara announced, checking her watch.

"Already? Time flies by here," Adam stated. "That reminds me, what exactly is your daily work schedule?"

"Usually the same as yours, I just stay late a lot of the time, to make sure everything is running smoothly. If I'm not working too hard, and just helping out, then I clock out and stick around. Sometimes I just play video games here, instead of at my apartment. I guess I just like the active environment," she explained. "Do you have your bags all packed?"

"Are you kicking me out?" Adam asked in sarcastic suspicion.

She gave him a playful smile and nudged shoulders with him. "No, silly, for the trip."

"We're going on a trip?"

"I didn't tell you? I can't believe this slipped my mind... The whole office is going to the grand opening of Machine Mountain. We're leaving in an hour on the company bus, and then staying at a hotel there for two nights."

"I read about it in the paper... The theme park is like living in the future, where everything is automated - electronically controlled," Adam said, remembering what he had read.

"The hotel is located directly in the middle of the park. Also, and this is the best part, guests of the hotel have exclusive access to the park, and the rides, all night long," she finished in excitement.

"I'll go pack now then."

It was a sunny day, and the traffic was flowing quickly. Adam walked alongside Lara, completely content with his life. The next few years were a mystery to him, but now, he felt safe and in control of his life for once. He had a chance with the girl of his dreams, and he wasn't going to let it get away from him.

They came to the crosswalk, where the pedestrian signal gave them the clear to walk across. However, the traffic light above them showed otherwise. Lara stepped into the street and began walking across, when Adam saw the speeding cars, who were only following the traffic signal's instructions.

In the split second he had, he grabbed her wrist and pulled her into his chest. One of the cars that drove through the intersection was t-boned by a car that was driving parallel to their direction, which also had a green light. When all was still, the pedestrian signal began flashing the stop hand, and the traffic lights flashed orange.

Lara looked at Adam in shock. She was a second away from death.

"This street has never done that before," Lara said.

"That's... weird."

Chapter 16: Adam

"Wow, that's a lot of luggage for two nights," I pointed out.

"Oh yeah," she blushed. "I'm just like every other girl in that way, I always have to bring half my closet."

"Is that bag solely for shoes?" I joked, nodding toward the tallest bag.

"No, that has my travel Playstation 3, Xbox 360 and Wii in it, with some hand held systems and travel games. And this one," she motioned toward the second largest, "has my travel server, for, well, you know."

I didn't know.

"And the second to the smallest has my four travel laptops, for PC gaming. The smallest contains my computer emergency kit. That thing has saved me more times than I can remember."

"Where do you keep your clothes?" I asked in disbelief.

"Oh, I have a change of clothes in my backpack." She picked up the very small, very pink backpack. "What are you bringing?"

For the first time, I was embarrassed of being normal. "Some clothes and sun block. I could bring some games though," I offered.

She smiled at my effort. "I have more than enough for us. Besides, I installed an entertainment system on the back of all the seats in the bus, which is connected to its own satellite network. That way, whenever our office goes on trips, we all play huge matches in games. My luggage is mainly for my hotel room."

"Is everyone a gamer at Jericho Communications?"

"Everyone is a gamer at heart."

We were dying. The A.I. had zeroed in on our location, and they were literally picking us off, one by one. Ken, the head of the graphic design department, was the first to go. We had no idea that the A.I. were with us before that. They were assassins in the night, with an unbelievably good aim.

"Danny!" Lara shouted, running to Dan's now still corpse. "I've let you down. I've let you all down."

I looked around the thrashed war field, guarding Lara as she mourned the loss of our fallen comrades. There were dead teammates on the ground of vibrant green grass, mixed with bright red embers. The suburbs were in ruins. The sky, grey with constant flocks of robot drop ships and their smog, and sea polluted with war ships.

"We have to go now, before they come back!" I advised in a hushed voice.

Lara picked up her gun, jaw clenched with fury. "Let's kick some tin ass."

We heard a team of heavy footsteps in a tunnel, under the pathway we were atop. Before I could jump down and unload my entire magazine on the bots, Lara held my trigger hand gently, and looked at me in the eyes. They told me not to act - it's what they expected.

I nodded and followed her. Behind a tree, off the pathway, and to the left of the tunnel that the bots travelled through, she lay in a prone position, setting her sights just after the opening. She signaled for me to station my machine gun just above the tunnel. I saw her flash a sly smile, before changing her crosshairs, from the tunnel, to me.

My cell phone began to vibrate viciously. The font was in a dripping blood style.

Look behind you :) - Wade

I turned and saw Wade in a robot suit, standing behind me with his never-ending smile. He lifted his death-laser rifle to my face. Before he was able to pull the trigger, a bullet broke through his armor, directly into his circuit-filled heart.

I looked back over at Lara and saw the smoke coming from the end of her barrel. The three A.I. from the tunnel ran out at her, guns blazing. She covered her head and tried to stay as perfectly still as she could. They knew she was there from the sound of her gun - they didn't, however, know I was standing directly above them.

I squeezed the trigger on Martin, Irene and Aurora, and yelled out a battle roar.

"Ahhhhhhh!" I yelled out in a battle roar.

The entire bus turned and looked at me as I fired with my mouse. My phone vibrated again.

Embarrassing... - Wade

Our fallen comrades were already playing a new game, as Lara and I were taking too long playing against my four friends. It just happened to be that the game involved humans under attack from space robots. Lara took the game very seriously, and in turn, so did I. It was extremely fun.

"Your friends are amazing. They killed everyone but us," she praised. "Where are they from?"

"Computers," I slipped out. "I mean, I met them from my computer... through the internet. They're from New York City."

"Maybe we can go on a trip to New York City and meet them."

"Well, they're not *that* good of friends," I said in an attempt to dissuade her.

HEY! That's cruel. - Wade

Machine Mountain seemed close, despite only having travelled an hour away from Jericho Communications. In this amount of time, I received dozens of text messages from Wade, Martin and Irene. They seemed to be past their Circuitry Board fear, except for Aurora. She wanted no part in communicating with me directly, and she also wanted Lara completely ignorant to the A.I. world. As much as I tried to tell myself otherwise, I felt she was right; I had the lingering unease of how in control the A.I. enforcement were.

The wind blew against the bus, pushing it a lane over. Food slid off our plates and between seats. Our entire plates would have gone overboard, without Lara's handy work. The small tables that unfolded from the back of each seat were made of metal, and the bottom of the plates, made of magnets. There was a small flaw in this though - the metal silverware stuck to the plates. With each shovel with a spoon, lifting it required a certain amount of force, which, even with the steadiest of hands, flung the food upward a bit. A small amount of each bite fell back down to the plate. It was an easy fix with plastic utensils, but no one ever thought to pack them.

A violent snow whipped across the highway. The passengers saw a bleak future at Machine Mountain, and forecasted their stay short, with a snowed-in amusement park. Co-workers, one by one, began falling helplessly asleep, expecting to turn around and head home.

"We're here!" Lara exclaimed in excitement.

Moans of the sleep depraved filled the bus, and they began subconsciously getting up and dragging their belongings behind them, filling up to the front of the bus. The windows were iced over, except the areas the windshield wiper scraped away. Each person was wearing their warmest clothing, and was shaking from the mere thought of stepping outside the toasty bus.

The door opened, and Lara and I, being the first ones to the front, got the brunt of the crisp air that blew past and quickly circulated the stuffy bus. We were all surprised to find that there was very little snowfall, and the wind was tame. Along Machine Mountain, the large steel hill, a constant *whirr* of fans fought against the snowstorm around the theme park. The fans were the size of propellers on a helicopter, and were constantly shifting for the finest weather suppression. They would crane up, and rotate around, to adapt to the wind change. When the snow and wind would calm, a couple of the fans would withdraw and fold into the metal hill.

It looked as though we were in an oddly shaped snow globe, except most of the snow was outside.

"That is the most amazing thing I've ever seen," Ronald, a fellow data analyst said, gaping up at the automated devices.

"I read about them from Machine Mountain's head engineer's blog. He says that is just a hint of what's to come," Lara explained in awe. "There are videos floating around the internet from people passing by and recording Machine Mountain doing test runs of the WindBlades."

Only small amounts of snow strayed from its school, and it fell like a calm winter day.

Lara and I continued on to the portcullis front entrance. Above it, read the sign *Machine Mountain.* And below it, *Don't touch the gate, please.* It had what seemed like electricity running through the bars, giving the gate life. I reached out to touch it, and it gave me a stern shock. An army of guns protruded from the panels on the walls, all different shapes and sizes, and all aiming at me. They ranged from machine guns, shotguns, handguns and even a bow and arrow.

"Your Machine Mountain passes please," a voice requested merrily from the speakers. "Ahh, Mr. Netak! Good to see you again. Welcome to Machine Mountain!" The electricity continued to flow through the gate as it lifted.

Despite there being over two dozen co-workers behind us, each gun kept their aim trained on me. It was a bit exciting. When I was out of site, each gun took aim on new a target. All the Jericho Communication tech nerds were giddy about being a target. Lara was one of them.

When the gateway lifted, and we entered, we walked into a dimly lit area. For a minute it seemed like a small snowy village - until it came to life. At each of our feet, two small lights on the ground drew apart, creating a circle around each of us, and then a fade of the light filled it. I looked around, and we all had the circle marker underneath us, each a different color than the other. Mine was a dark green, while Lara's, a steel blue.

It confused us all, as to how the lights even operated. The ground, along with the portcullis, had the metallic look of steel. How light escaped from the surface puzzled us.

We were all excited about the rings of light under us, that we forgot about the rest of the park for the moment. Even Mr. Netak tried jumping away from his large orb of light. He couldn't outsmart it.

Lamps glowed with light that faded the further they went. Shops had the texture of brick or stone, with small windows covered by curtains. It definitely wasn't what any of us were expecting. It seemed like a fifteenth century town.

"So, this *tavern* we're to sleep in is in the middle of Camelot?" Ben, the funny guy of the office, asked sarcastically.

Most of the people laughed, but immediately stopped when a bright light powered on down the road. The machine was the size and shape of a soccer ball. Just eight feet in the air, it hung like a piñata.

It suddenly zoomed over to us, hanging from a strong power cord. One optical lens looked out through the opening of one of the sides. Instead of the gadget turning for the camera to look in other directions, the camera lens only shifted in the machine, and the panel it once looked through, closed, and another panel side opened where the camera lens poked out to look through.

As it passed the shops, the walls changed from stone and brick walls, to glass walls and cathode lights, which gleamed on the merchandise. The walls, the floor, and even some of the windows changed theme, instantly. We were now in a dark futuristic city.

The hanging device stopped at our group, and opened five of its many sides at once, so the optical lens could move and look freely at our entire group. "Welcome to Machine Mountain! I'm Vern, your Machine Mountain Resort exclusive guide," the friendly ball said in an auto-tuned voice. "Charge complete!"

The cord it hung from disconnected, and Vern fell two feet, before a whir of fans sounded from the bottom of it. The bottom ports had opened, revealing fans that spun to keep it steadily in the air. When it lost balance and tipped over to the side, it repositioned the open panels, to go along with the fans, and it continued hovering.

My co-workers received a surge of energy after seeing the first few surprises Machine Mountain had to offer, and instead of following Vern, the hovering robot, they ventured out into the futuristic fun land. I was ready to join them, when I noticed that Lara seemed half-awake. Her eyes were dark, and she had a soda in her hand and continued gulping it down, to stay awake.

She revealed to me that she was very excited for the theme park, too excited, in fact, that she spent the past night researching the park online, with no sleep. Still, she took my hand and pulled to explore Machine Mountain, like a stubborn child. I told her I wanted to get sleep and then see every attraction the next day. She surrendered, and retreated to her room.

And, as fast as the night started, it ended. However, not before I met my new roommate.

The contents of my luggage were already sorted into the dresser on my side of the room. The drawers only needed a touch to slide open automatically. I wondered how it worked, as I only put it in a conveyor belt that Vern told us to put our luggage on. I touched the top drawer, which slid open, containing all my clothes. I didn't need to look in the others, but I was curious anyway.

The second drawer contained an eBook reader, which had dozens of bibles installed on it. The last drawer I opened, had more clothes. They weren't mine though. They were all small and bright colors. I picked one up and, viewing it away from the rest, realized it was sexy lingerie. Very sexy and very skimpy.

"What do you think you're doing?" a voice came from behind me.

I turned around to find a supermodel in a towel, coming out of the bathroom. At that moment, the lights dimmed, the two twin beds formed together, two glasses of wine sank from a panel connected to the ceiling and smooth jazz began playing, seemingly from nowhere. As I stood, blameless, she looked at me as if I were the scum of the earth.

After I explained myself and put back the lingerie - the jazz fizzled, the beds detached and the lights shined. As the two of us laughed it off, and drank our wine, two robotic claws reached down from the ceiling and took our glasses, while I was in mid sip.

Eight hours later, I awoke to Lara's joyful smile. She had been staring at me for five minutes, wanting to not wake me, until she *accidently* coughed very loudly.

The ceiling was in disarray. The panel from where the wine lowered was open, with a jack wedged between to keep it ajar. My roommate lay half-dressed, on top of her covers, with an empty bottle of wine she cradled tightly to her chest in one hand, and a crowbar loosely in the other.

"What happened to her?"

"She's Sally, Jericho Communications' mechanic, and our drunk," Lara answered, unfazed by the scene.

She sure didn't look like a mechanic of any kind.

We never stayed in the same place for too long, as Lara wanted to see the entire park in an instant. We rode on the Wheels of Steel; solved the Circuit Trap; conquered the Plasma Planet; and fished out a solar powered electric eel from the Memory Pool. Apparently, I was the first person to have won a robotic sea creature all day. I even got my picture taken by other Machine Mountain visitors... But now that I think back on it, they may have just wanted to have taken a picture of the strange prize.

When we grew hungry, we spotted a moving popcorn cart. The speakers from the cart played songs you might hear in a sci-fi movie. String instruments played gently, until the tune sped up and synthesizers took over. The smell of the melting butter on the popping kernels was irresistible to us and we hailed it to a halt.

A family a few feet away ordered two small buckets. The popped popcorn was fluffy, and lightly buttered and lightly salted, as those were the options the family chose. It looked lightly delicious.

Lara's stomach made such a mighty roar, that I thought it could've attacked the buckets and claimed the kill for itself. She charged the cart before it could wheel away, and ordered one of the largest buckets of popcorn she could. For the options, she selected the same as the family moments ago.

The robotic hands quickly went to work, scooping up the golden treat, salting it and finally buttering it. I could feel the heat from the popcorn and butter radiate out around it, and Lara and I took swift bites. It wasn't long before we were coughing it up. The popcorn was drenched in butter.

"That's enough salt and butter in there to give an army a heart attack," I said hoarsely, as the salted butter scratched through my throat.

It was strange, and for a moment I couldn't believe it, but as the cart wheeled away, it sang passionately, "Killing me softly."

Chapter 17: Wade

"A.I. visitors of Machine Mountain: there has been a security breach, and I'm sorry to inform you that I will be cutting all communications in and out of our network. Our service will be back up after the affair is sorted," the auto-tuned voice said.

I let out a disappointed groan as soon as the connection closed.

Aurora and I were waiting as Lara flagged down a popcorn cart. Afterward we could follow them into more rides and attractions, however the connection to Machine Mountain blocked us out.

"I knew we should have kept going without our users."

Aurora showed a concerned frown. "I hope Vern will be alright," she said.

"Who?" I asked, without caring what the answer was.

I was begrudging the fact that I would have to use Adam's cell phone camera to look through again. The Machine Mountain interface allowed A.I. to view the theme park from the walls and ground; virtually, most of the surface. While Aurora and I were following Adam and Lara around the park, Martin and Irene decided to go off on their own. Many of the A.I. from Jericho Communications were also wandering around the

Machine Mountain servers, gawking at all the new technology, along with a countless amount of other A.I., all excited for the grand opening.

"Vern is the Machine Mountain conductor. He controls just about everything that goes on there. Well, the users who created Machine Mountain programmed his system to do that," she answered, with stars in her eyes. "He is said to be the most advanced supercomputer to date, and even planted some of the inventions in his users' heads sneakily, by revealing the formulas subliminally - to make Machine Mountain possible."

"Vern... Vern... Wait, the bodiless robot that floats around the theme park?" I asked, remembering the strange little machine.

"Yes. He's so intelligent and cares so much for the users in his park," she stated dreamily. "That security breach is probably fixed by now, he's just patching up the security hole to keep the users safe in Machine Mountain, I'm sure."

"Sounds like you want this Vern to be your Vern."

"Oh, no, it wouldn't be possible. He most likely has lines of thousands of A.I., who are much more eligible. Although..." she drifted off in thought. I could only imagine what she was daydreaming about. It would have something to do with this valiant Vern and his godlike features, noticing Aurora, out of a horde of A.I., and making her queen of Machine Mountain. "Of course I will be your queen..." she muttered airily.

In the main quarters of her ship, a door in the deck grew to be ten times its length, and the head A.I. of Jericho began piling inside. They were all different shapes and sizes. Some of them were like Martin, they appeared as stick figures, except more detailed. It was an easy guess to say their users had boring jobs, like data analysts. Some were like me, where they took the form of a human, and others had their avatars to look how I used to, a single image. A surprising amount were like Aurora, with her motherboard skin; PCI-E slots, CPUs, capacitors, jumpers, cache chips, etc.

"Sorry for barging in with so many, Aurora, but we're here for the fugitive," the leader informed. He looked like an old and wise A.I., much older than five years. I would later find out that he was the A.I. on Mr. Netak's computer.

"Damn it, Wade," Aurora spat, angry that I ruined her daydream.

"Wade, if you'll come with us," the leader said in more of an order than anything else.

"What's going on?" I asked, not trying to play the fool, but I was truly confused. "Shouldn't it be the CBA after me?"

"We don't let the CBA into Jericho, but when we get a fugitive in our midst, we do cooperate with them. You're going to come with us and turn yourself in. They will give you a better sentence that way. We have your accomplice, Martin, in stasis."

"A better sentence? Instead of complete destruction of my system, they will just wipe my memory?" I asked coldly. "I'll pass. I broke a broken law. I'd rather seclude myself from the internet forever, than go to the CBA." Without Aurora's help and the A.I. Guardian's protection, I wouldn't be able to sneak online without repercussions.

"You broke a broken law? What exactly happened?" he asked, still keeping a hard face.

"Willard," Aurora addressed Mr. Netak's A.I. "He contacted his user to help him. As it wasn't a violent crime, and because my user has a soft spot for Wade's user, I hoped you could hear him out, at least."

"Even though it wasn't a violent crime, it doesn't make it any less serious. Never communicate with users, that is the first law. However, if we remove and disable your system from being able to contact your user ever again-" he explained, until I cut him off.

"No, I'll never stop talking to Adam, and I wouldn't take it back for the life of me. He was going to commit suicide, and Martin and I sent him a text message to try to stop him. He jumped anyway, and he was still extremely depressed afterward, and we tried to cheer him up without contacting him. We put subtle stuff on the ads of websites he would frequent, and small things like that. It never seemed to work though, and he continued to get worse.

"The text message, though, the CBA must have caught onto it, because they sent a bounty hunter after Martin and I. I disconnected from the internet in time, but not Martin. The bounty hunter took him, and I didn't know what to do, or how to track him.

"That's when I made the second contact with Adam," I continued. "I asked him to, actually, break into Jericho Communications, so I could get past your firewall and get the IP address of the bounty hunter. That's when Adam met Lara, and he was happy for the first time in months. He's now in love with her. I'm not going to accept any fate, other than to see out what happens between those two," I finished stubbornly.

Most of the women, and a few of the men inside the living room, began getting teary eyed. Even Willard started sniffling and holding back a tear.

"That's the most beautiful thing I've ever heard," one of the stick figure A.I. said emotionlessly.

"Screw the CBA, they want in, they can lay siege!" Willard exclaimed with a smile.

"Wait," Aurora said, confused. "He committed a crime; we could all be in danger now."

The crowd was quick to boo her.

"You're saying you want to give him up to the CBA?" Willard asked.

"Well, no. But I don't think he deserves a damn medal for contacting Adam - he still jumped!" Lara argued.

She only received more boos.

It wasn't until later that night that Adam called me, in the presence of Aurora and Willard... and even Lara.

Chapter 18: Adam

It was quiet for the first time that day. Lara and I laid on our backs, side by side, fingers locked. We were on a floating cloud, gazing up into the stars, and at the moon that looked back down on us. I turned my head and looked at Lara, who was watching the other clouds in the sky. Her silhouette looked like beautiful mountains blocking out the stars. I would have kissed her if my mouth didn't taste like salt and butter.

The ride, Cloud Computing, didn't stop unless we commanded it to, for there was no line. The theme park closed a couple hours ago, and we were lying on this saucer for what felt like an hour. On the saucer was a material that felt softer than a down comforter did. I wasn't sure what was holding it up, but it moved so subtly and unpredictably, that when we would look down, we would be in an entirely different location in the astronomy section of Machine Mountain.

The giant fans were retracted, as there was only a cool breeze and harmless clouds. We would occasionally spot a couple of Jericho Communications employees roaming the lot under us.

"Sally and I should build one of these for the office," Lara proposed. "I think I would be more productive on one of these. That or I wouldn't lack sleep ever again." We shared a laugh, and she sat up to look down on Machine Mountain once again. She pointed at someone walking out of the Star Bar next door. "Look, its Philip - my roommate!"

I sat up quickly and peered down. Philip isn't a woman's name, I noted. There he was, hair black as a raven and eyes as green and bright as an emerald on a sunny night. His features: chiseled.

"I haven't seen him around the office," I said, trying to remember him at Jericho Communications.

"Oh, he doesn't work with us."

"What?" I asked, as someone from our office should have been sharing a room with her instead, preferably, me.

"He was my prom date about seven years ago."

"What?!?"

"My dad invited him," she told me.

It suddenly made sense. "Of course he did."

We were tumbling off the saucer the next moment. I only had a split second to grab hold of both the short safety rail along the sides, and Lara's wrist. The platform began to rotate left and right violently, in random repetitions, twisting my wrist. However, I was able to keep a firm grip, on both the rail and Lara. The fall that seemed eminent was easily seven stories. The ride was trying to throw us off.

Lara looked up and saw that I was straining to hold us up. "Adam, you can climb down if you let me go," Lara pointed out, but in a scared voice.

"No."

"Hello, may I help you find your way back to your rooms?" an auto-tuned voice came whirring quickly up to our dangle.

"Yes! Please, we need this cloud thing to take us back to the ground!" I said eagerly.

The robot shook its fish eye lens back and forth. "Cloud Computing is currently under maintenance. If you will please exit the platform, we will get you back to your room in Machine Mountain Resort in no time," he said in his auto-tuned voice.

Lara and I both looked down and saw cold steel seventy feet below. "I don't think the robot realizes we're this high off the ground," she said with fright in her voice. "I'd like to talk to your operator," she requested.

"Uhhh, oh yes, right," Vern said. The auto-tune in his speech disappeared, leaving a quick and nervous voice coming out of the speakers. "This is the operator speaking... Lloyd. Oh, I see the predicament you're in. If you just let go, there is a safety net below."

"I don't see it," Lara said, looking down.

"It's clear, new technology," he convinced.

"Wait... Lloyd?" *Another first name.* I haven't known A.I. with a last name. "What's your last name?"

"Kevin, my last name is Kevin," he said quickly.

He *has* to be A.I.

Come to think of it, this isn't the first time in these past few days machines have tried to do Lara and I harm. There was the traffic lights, which Lara said have never made an error before, and the popcorn. Of course, the latter was more subtle harm. And now, the saucer is trying to shake us off.

"You're working for the CBA!" I accused Vern.

"I'd never!" he denied.

"And that proves that you're A.I., which makes you that much more possible to be working with them. How else would you know what the CBA is?"

"It is," he began, pausing to gather his thoughts. "the Charles Bronson Admirers."

"Then why would you never be a part of that?" I spat. "It sounds awesome!"

"What's going on?" Lara asked, befuddled.

"I don't have time for this," Vern said. He kept the side of where his camera lens was, half open, and then began ramming his head against my hand.

"Stop that!" I shouted.

"Let go!" he demanded.

He backed up quite a bit, to gather speed and hit my fingers. When that didn't work, he opened a few of his little sliding doors, hovered to have a finger or two inside the bays and closed them, clamping down on my fingers. Next, with my fingers clamped, he tried prying my hand off the safety bar. He was far too light to use any type of force on me, however.

"Alright, I didn't want to do this, but you asked for it. Just hold on while I recharge," he said and then the hanging cord came from seemingly nowhere and connected like a magnet to the top side of his head, where he opened a port for it. We waited, in that idle state, for a couple of minutes.

"Adam, what is the CBA? What do you mean about A.I.?" Lara asked as we waited for Vern to recharge.

"If I tell you, I fear you'll be in danger," I answered gravely.

"How much more dangerous can it get?" she laughed lightly.

She had a point, so I told her everything: about the woman I had a crush on; my boss giving me my two weeks' notice, to give to him; the two of them together; the text message sent by A.I., and finally, the jump. I also told her about my A.I. friends, Wade, Martin and Irene, and her A.I., Aurora. Then, I told her about our enemies, the CBA and the bounty hunters. I could see that the part about how I wasn't really tree climbing hurt her, because she frowned, causing her chin to crinkle, but she continued to listen. When I was done, I told her that I didn't want to lie to her, but I couldn't betray my friends.

"Adam, I understand. It's the classic eighties plot. Anyone who's seen an eighties kids movie would understand: *you know something that you shouldn't*," she said and sighed. "I just liked it a lot when I thought you were a tree climber."

"I can climb more trees," I promised.

This would have been the part where we kissed, but she was out of range. Instead, I gave her a smile and she gave my leg a soft hug with her other arm.

"My charge is complete," he said, and a sudden bolt of electricity shot out from his front panel and struck me in the chest.

I passed out for a moment, only to kick and wake up and find myself falling down, further and further. Lara held my hand tightly as we crashed into a transparent net about ten feet above the building of Gravity Ball. The net lowered, by four poles holding the net in place, until we were safely on the roof.

Vern dropped from the sky, and then opened his bottom sides to hover again. "I told you I don't work for the CBA. Now, hurry, before they catch up," he ordered trying to lead us forward.

"I think we're pretty safe up here for now," I pointed out.

"I think not," Lara said, pointing up at one of the saucers being rocked like a wrecking ball toward us. "Run!"

We, then, gladly followed Vern. He led us off Gravity Ball, down an escalator, which tried to reroute its direction into a sewer pit that opened from the ground. Vern flew into the escalator we were on, between two steps and pushed a step up, overriding the system to do an emergency shutdown on the escalator. We went down the steps and jumped to the right of the sewer opening, and exited the Astronomy district.

"Don't you control the park?" Lara asked Vern.

"Yes, but they intruded and are quickly taking over everything. They can't control me, but they can control the park, and I was only able to cut them off from the shopping area."

"That's the entrance! Then we can get out!" Lara said excitedly.

"We have to make it there first."

"What about the rest of Jericho Communications? My dad?" she asked.

"I overheard the A.I. in my system saying that they're only after one person, Priority One User, otherwise known as, Adam. However, I believe you, Ms. Netak, is also in danger, as they have been observing the two of you tonight and noted they can use you, to get to Adam."

"How are we going to get out? Everything seems to be able to move and transform, even the ground."

"All you have to do is follow my lead," he answered.

It was as simple as that. He led us through a maze of rides, underground maintenance rooms, and automated security detail. He knew Machine Mountain like the back of his hand... or the back of his coding. He explained, on the way, that the CBA shut down all cell towers in the area, to complete the trap, so I couldn't call for help.

"You're not afraid of the CBA?" I asked.

"Not as afraid as I am of getting shut down. I have as strong a security as I can have, allowing only the exception of the CBA. However, once they divulged their plan to stage your death as an accident in my park, I couldn't allow that. Think about it, if a user were to be injured during the opening weekend of Machine Mountain, the theme park would be disassembled and trashed. I would be torn to pieces!" Vern exclaimed. "Here we are."

We ducked into a shop. Inside was lined with an assortment of self-defense weapons. You couldn't actually use any of the products, as they were enclosed behind thick glass. Most were available to buy online, with the exceptions of the illegal and prototype weapons, which were only for display. Metal hands were in each of the cases, activating the weapons occasionally. One of the robotic hands triggered a stun gun behind Lara, making her jump.

"Do either of you know how to use a gun?" Vern asked.

"I don't think guns work against A.I."

Vern hovered toward the metal wall. Suddenly the wall became as transparent as glass; however, I noticed something as I stood so close to it - the wall was pixelated. With the excitement and constant motion during the day, I never noticed that the walls, the ground, and just about every surface that changed its appearance in Machine Mountain, were electronic visual displays. I touched it and it felt as cold and smooth as metal.

"I wasn't referring to using them against A.I., I was talking about *them*," he said, nodding at the wall, where a team of about two dozen men with automatic guns patrolled outside. "The Circuitry Board's outside agents."

"Can they see us?" Lara's voice shuddered slightly. She pulled me close, and tried to guide me behind cover with her, despite the lack of solid objects to hide behind.

"No, I made the wall to appear as if this store was empty."

Outside, a man bigger than Mr. Netak led the men, and stopped to turn around, which made his men fumble and quickly realign in a military formation. He wore a patrol hat tightly around his head, a tough black and grey jacket with large pockets, and a pistol on his hip. He gave them all a sour look.

"Cop Seventeen assigned me with the lot of you," he said with disgust in his mouth. "His reasoning was simple. You are all idiots. You share that with Priority One User. Cop Five Ninety-one spotted the target enter this shopping center. You will split into three groups; two at the exits of the shopping center, and the third searching one shop at a time."

"Yes sir, Agent Two!" they all exclaimed simultaneously.

The next few moments were a mess. They all lowered their guns with one arm and started picking teams. A few would disagree - that they didn't believe they should be parts of certain teams. Others wanted to play rock-paper-scissors for the best shooter among them. Agent Two groaned and put a stop to it. He began shoving the men, with ease, into three directions, out of random. After they were sorted, they saluted him, and carried out their duties.

The group sent on patrol, charged into the closest store. There was silence about a minute, until we heard gunfire, screaming from both the store, and through the radios, and Agent Two shouting back in the radios. He never got an answer of what attacked them.

"That takes care of one group," Vern said successfully.

"You." Agent Two pointed at shortest operative, who looked behind him to see who he was pointing at. "Go to the mainframe and shut off the power grid to the shopping district. Agent Five Ninety-one will direct you on how to kill the power."

"I had a feeling they were going to take this course of action," Vern stated. He hovered around the room, unlocking each weapon's case wirelessly. "Take any you'd like. The users that run Machine Mountain will figure that the government seized them after this mess. They did, after all, pay for their production."

The most out of place weapon was a pair of sunglasses and two handguns. "What do these do?" I asked, as I slid the glasses on.

The only thing I could see, was the store's floor. I couldn't see anything else, no matter where I looked, until Vern asked Lara to hand me the two pistols that went with the shades. When she moved the pistols into my hands, I saw my feet. I held the guns up and aimed them, no, looked through them, in front of me, behind me, and on my left and right. The lenses looked through the cameras on the guns. I could see two places at once, and it made me a bit dizzy.

"Go ahead, fire a test shot. This model is unloaded," Vern urged me.

Despite the gun being unloaded, I aimed it at the floor, and fired the weapon. It sent a strong surge of electricity through my arm and I let go of it like a cat jumping from water.

"Oh well, it was worth a shot. That model is currently being tested on one Clyde Creedence. They must have enabled a security feature that allows only him to fire the weapon."

I removed the sunglasses and then picked up a prototype rifle.

"That's a fine choice, indeed," Vern praised. "The *General Lightning Gun 20*, otherwise known as, the GLG20. It fires both a single bolt, and a chain bolt of electricity. The setting is right there on a safety switch."

I looked near my index finger, to find a knob, which pointed at an S, for safety, in white paint. Above it, three bolts of lightning, one after the other, and above that, a single bolt, all in red paint.

"You just need to make certain, if it is set to a chain bolt, that *only* your targets are in front of you. Who knows what could happen in that 180-degree angle. Now, load up on weaponry, you'll need it. Good. Now, shut your eyes and cover them. We only have one shot at this, so be ready!"

Even with my eyes shut tightly, a blinding light filled my vision, and I dropped two of the guns I was carrying to cover my eyes in pain. Vern had made all the walls let out a blinding white light.

"Go and shoot! The guns are non-lethal, so don't hesitate."

Lara took a hand I was using to cover my eyes, and led me out of the shop. More than a dozen men, including Agent Two, were shielding their eyes, or putting their hands out to feel for something, anything. One of the agents found his way to their leader, and Agent Two smacked his soldier's hands away, and squinted at Lara and I.

"Straight ahead, fire!" he ordered, lifting his own gun.

I lifted mine, set it to chain bolt with my right index finger, and fired. An erratic strand of electricity shot from the barrel, and jumped from CBA agent to CBA agent. Those that were hit, fell to the floor, shaking and stuttering. There were a few others left, but my gun could only then fire single bolts, as the yellow LED indicator light showed the battery was low.

Lara shot a few rounds of tranquilizer darts that put a pair of agents down into a heavy doze. She even shot Agent Two in the arm, but he only pulled the dart out and threw it to the ground. He was about to lift his gun and shoot more, as his sight was better, but his arm was fast asleep. Before he could lift his right hand and pull his trigger finger using his left, Lara and I made a break for the exit.

The group at guard were about to open fire, when all of the lights shut down. The only light that appeared were single bolts of lightning I shot that struck the unsuspecting guards. The gate began lowering, and Lara guided me to it. I continued to fire and Lara was now on the other side yelling for me to follow.

They could still shoot through the gate. I had to take out as many of them as I could before joining her.

"Top left! To the right!" Lara assisted, shooting her own dart gun at the guards.

I looked around at my handiwork and noticed that the LED light was a fading red. In that moment, I was so pleased with myself, that I began laughing triumphantly.

"Hurry, it's almost closed!" Lara rushed.

"Oh, right!" I slid most skillfully under the lowering gate. My unkempt hair, however, didn't make it in time. The portcullis enclosed tightly and I shrieked like a girl. The electricity from the gate was charging through my hair and tingling my scalp. "Help! Help!" I called out helplessly.

Lara unsheathed a knife from her boot and cut my pinned hair free. The knife's handle was decorated with videogame characters. I leaned up with an elbow, felt my lopsided hair and decided it was a good time to get a haircut anyway.

"You carry a knife in your boot?" I asked in awe.

"I figure that Jack Burton would always say-"

Before she could finish, I kissed her. That's right, we finally kissed. While she still supported my head with one hand, we kissed. I've never felt more in love.

Chapter 19: Aurora

Lara had already met Wade, Martin and Irene. My system lay on the coffee table, in front of Adam and Lara. It was used as the terminal for the meeting. In my webcam, Lara looked to be in constant anticipation, while Adam looked delighted to introduce his A.I. to her.

Wade couldn't stand still before she met them; he was either pacing while he waited, or asking Martin if he should change his avatar to be something a little more welcoming. Martin was at ease, and waited patiently. Me, I stood just to the right of Martin, invisible to them all.

"Maybe a clown fish - users love clown fish," Wade tried convincing.

"I think you should just be yourself," Martin suggested.

In that moment, Wade's avatar boxed in to form his computer case. "I feel a bit square, like this."

"Like yourself - like you usually are," Martin corrected him.

He then transformed into his usual humanoid avatar, except with larger muscles and a smoldering look on his face. Martin shook his head in disappointment, but said nothing.

She had already known them by name, as Adam told her all about us, on the taxi ride home from Machine Mountain.

"Lara, there is one last person I'd like you to meet," Adam began. "And I know she wants to meet you more than anyone in the world."

Despite not programming myself to blush, I felt as though all the eyes were on me, despite being invisible, and that my red cheeks could show my nervousness. I revealed myself, although just as a stutter at first. I flickered in and out of sight, as my emotions were in control.

During these long years, I've dedicated my life to Lara. I know everything about her. I have even helped her. I've blocked dirty websites that she accidently clicked on; vanquished viruses; guided her on the right path; and I was even her DJ when she set her music to random. She has always been my best friend, except, I had just then realized that I have never spoken a word to her. It was frightening.

What do you say to someone that you have wanted to talk to since your first spark of existence?

"Aurora?" Lara called out. Her eyes searched the computer screen. She continued to speak, "As soon as Adam said your name, I remembered the video game I began creating before I worked at Jericho Communications. I named the heroine of the video game, *Aurora*."

"That's where I got my name from," I said, and finally allowed them to see me. "As well as my appearance."

Lara's eyes brightened. "You're just as I wanted to create her!" she exclaimed.

"After you created the draft of the 3D model, I borrowed your concept art and finished it," I told. "I also continued making the game after you started working at Jericho Communications."

"That is amazing, Aurora," she commended.

"It is in its beta process, and it still needs a lot more work. I would need your help on most of it." I felt shy, but I realized that Lara would accept me, no matter what. She was kind. "You can play it, if you would like to."

"Can I play it with you?"

I felt my system flutter with relief. She wants to play the video game with me!

"Yes, it would take a few days, but I can make it playable for all of us," I said, and then rose my nose to Wade and Adam. "I'll just have to give them a handicap, since they aren't as good as us."

"Please," Wade said with distaste. "Adam and I can destroy both of you till you plead to go back to playing house in your sissy games."

"I believe I kicked your ass last time a scoreboard was in the equation."

"That time wasn't fair!"

"Oh yeah?" I shouted and poked his burly chest. "Lara - let's show these noobs how it's done!"

Chapter 20: Adam

After I introduced Lara to the A.I., I found myself left out of many inside jokes. I saw her less as well, as she and Aurora worked on their video game together. Aurora, however, warmed up to me. She scolded me for getting Lara in danger, but, quickly after, told me how happy she was that Lara met me. Lara has been happier, she told me in private.

Wade spent most of his time boasting about our last video game match. He was so amped up, that he accidently killed me a few times, trying to shoot Aurora. In the end, he was the victor, and Aurora gave him brief congratulations and moved on. He never let it go.

As for Lara and I, we have never been closer. There was half a day when we held hands, the entire time. When one of us needed to type on the computer, we worked up a solution where we would say the word, then type it together. I would use my left hand on the left side of the keyboard, and Lara, her right, on the right side of the keyboard. Wade and Aurora suggested we could just ask them to enter what we wanted to type, but Lara and I had too much fun doing it our way.

We had a lot to do before we had to go back to work, however. We went shopping, researching, and contacted old friends, to figure out how to protect ourselves from the CBA's future attack, which we knew was coming. Lara's apartment wasn't in her name, that's why they haven't showed up at our door. But, across the street, we would occasionally see suspicious vans drive around Jericho Communications, and we knew, if we were to return, they would apprehend us.

Running was not an option for Lara. She loved her family and her job. I agreed. A month or two ago, I would have had no problem leaving, but with Lara, and at Jericho Communications, life was as I always wanted it. I even liked Lara's dad, despite him not having the highest opinion of me.

Therefore, we had to plan for several situations where we had to confront the CBA, both inside agents, and out.

"My dad says he will give us three days off, so we have to make them count," Lara said to the room.

It was an actual virtual chat room, with Wade, Martin, Irene, Aurora, and me. Three other people were in the room, sitting at the round table. We were introduced to their leader, Willard, the main administer of Jericho city. He was a quiet man, and looked to have been from the dawn of computers. He dressed in blue robes, as a wizard. Whenever Lara and I would speak, he would look up at us, and his tired eyes would have a new light that shined in them.

They were all in a system that wasn't occupied by A.I. - it hosted as a private meeting place of

Jericho A.I. The room echoed, as it looked to be a futuristic cathedral, with blue, yellow and red dim LED lights that lit up the corners, and schematic patterns glowing in stained glass. It was very peaceful, and even though Lara and I were looking through Aurora's monitor, we felt like we were there, sitting at the black, round marble table with them.

"I think we should get tracking devices and set them up in all of your systems," I suggested. "An old friend told me about them. They aren't too big. We can put them in the desktop cases."

"Yes," Willard agreed.

"I will order the tracking devices tonight, have them shipped to the office, and install one on every computer system in Jericho Communications. It's a good idea even if the CBA weren't after us," Lara announced, squeezing my hand.

"Isn't that a bit of an invasion of our privacy?" one of Willard's men argued.

Willard chortled. "Are you planning on going somewhere other than your desk?" he mocked. "We shall have tracking devices. A splendid plan."

An ancient computer liked our idea! I continued to tell myself to keep face, but I could feel the corners of my mouth giving me away.

"We will need to get into the office without the CBA knowing, though," Lara pointed out.

"With Adam's track record, I don't think he will have a problem accomplishing that," Aurora said bitterly.

"Irene and I can devise another plan!" Wade exclaimed excitedly. Aurora made a displeased snort, but he completely ignored it. "This time, maybe you can actually land on the roof."

"The infamous break in. You really caught us by surprise when you stole that information," Willard's right hand man said.

"What do we do about the outside agents?" Martin asked. "How will we stop them from apprehending Adam and Lara?"

There was a long pause before the first person spoke.

"How about we contact the local news when they make their move? The CBA won't want to be seen by them," Aurora inputted.

"We will need to be a step ahead of them," I said. "We will need to know when they will make their move."

"The vans that patrol the parking lot around the office - they might have computers in them. The A.I. of Jericho Communications can try to hack into them. They know that Willard won't allow them to take us, but they won't expect him to send an attack on their vans," Aurora finished, satisfied with her strategy.

"Task some of our men to scout for wireless connections outside Jericho Communications. Find the CBA agents," Willard ordered one of his men.

"What if they come in and, well, try to eliminate us?" I asked, starting to realize how surreal it all was. A government black-ops team was out for my neck. Mine. How strange...

"Bring some of the weapons that you acquired at Machine Mountain," Martin said. "To protect yourselves."

"You should also install security in the building," Irene added. "Such as armored doors that are computer controlled, and will go, 'faulty', to keep the CBA out, if just to slow them down."

"Vern could help us with that," Aurora said positively.

I wasn't so positive. "He might not be willing to help us, actually. When he saved Lara and I in Machine Mountain, he made it clear that if we died on opening weekend, they would shut him down, and that's why he helped us."

"Oh, so the valorous Vern was just trying to save his own neck?" Wade chuckled, attempting to pick a fight with Aurora.

"If he were to be deleted, then he wouldn't be able to bring happiness to millions of users hearts each year," she shot back.

"Oh yeah, I'm sure-" Wade began, but was cut short by explosions of fire streaming up to the ceiling, lasers pointing in synchronization and fog forming from the cathedral's port entrance.

"An attack! Defensive positions everyone!" Willard roared, pointing at the port.

The port, however, was now a stage, and the A.I. were in the front row of a huge audience. The audience were cheering and clapping around them. Every one of them was peculiar, however. They were textureless, and faceless, each one a different color. They were just animations - only decorations in the room.

On stage, rose from the floor, two A.I., one skinny, the other stubby. They raised their hands, to hush the cheers.

"Ladies and gentlemen," a British accent announced from a recording in the large speakers on stage. "We are proud to present the founders of, The Underground Resistance - TUR!"

"I'd like to thank my mum," said the stubby, British A.I., but was quickly elbowed in the ribs by the other. "What? Are we not doing that anymore?"

"Who are you, and how did you get into Jericho Communications?" Aurora demanded, still gathering her defenses to boot them out.

"Nelson and Todd," Todd introduced casually, motioning to his skinny friend and then himself. "When my cousin Bret knew his organization, Jericho, was fighting the CBA, he thought to include us. Oh, but, he told me not to say he referred us, so if you could forget that I told you that."

"Bret the Brit - I knew it was a mistake when Aaron imported that PC from Europe," Aurora growled scornfully.

The thinner British man stepped to the front of the stage. "Please, we want to help, in any way we can," Nelson said whole-heartedly.

"It's nice to meet you!" Lara greeted excitedly.

Nelson stood, frozen, looking up at her. He began to walk to the left side of the screen, never breaking contact with Lara eyes, and we followed him with our eyes. He then ran to the right of the screen, faked left, ran right some more, and then suddenly gasped.

"Everyone," he whispered. "Stay as quiet and still as you can. The users of this system can see us. We must act as if this is a viral video that they stumbled upon." Nelson thought we weren't supposed to see them, and tried taking control of the situation by tricking Lara and I into thinking we were watching a fictional video.

"One of us needs to do something hilarious," Wade encouraged, wide-eyed with enthusiasm. He wanted them to do something silly, I could tell. "Then they will *truly* think it is a viral video, and then we can send them on their way to a webpage... or something."

The two stood, as deer looking into headlights. We, including the rest of the chat room, watched Todd and Nelson, waiting for their plan to develop. Todd's face turned a bit red, as if under pressure, and then a long and quiet whisping sound came from behind him, as he rose one leg casually. The gas sound continued for a few seconds, never climaxing.

It seemed as though Wade's plan backfired, though, because instead of laughing, he just had an uncomfortable look on his face.

"I'm Lara, and this is Adam," Lara greeted, as if nothing had happened.

"Of course," Nelson said, realizing that we were the users who knew about A.I. "Bret told me about the two of you. It's a pleasure to meet you."

"Well, you know about them, what about you? I've never heard of The Underground Resistance," Aurora stated. With a few commands, the front row they were sitting at rotated into the round table again and the audience disappeared, along with the lasers and fog.

"Yes, we're *that* underground. We mostly do more subtle work, such as charities for those affected by the CBA," he informed.

"What can you offer us?"

"Right, why we are here... We have over one thousand A.I. freedom fighters, ready to join you in your cause," Nelson announced.

"One-thousand and six," Todd added.

"Although, some of our men have slow internet connections, or live out of the country."

"Ninety-one percent," Todd interrupted again.

Nelson gave his partner a cold stare before he continued in irritation. "Some of our men, like I said." He then scanned over us with a seriousness about him.

"And most of them aren't trained in the art of war," Todd made clear.

"Alright, fine! You give the presentation!" Nelson yelled, fed up with Todd interrupting him.

"I'm your partner - not your representative," he chuckled, as if absurd.

"Whatever," he said, all professionalism gone. "There you have it. We may not have an army and they may not be as trained and powerful and fast as the Jericho A.I. - but they're good A.I., ready to die for the cause."

"Except Glen - he's a proper tosser," Todd stated.

"Well, yes, Glen is a bit of an ass," his friend agreed quietly.

"Well, you sound like a group that can aid us. Welcome aboar..." Willard began, but paused as Nelson began flickering in a stasis. "Is he having internet difficulties?"

"Oh, it's nothing, he'll be back in no time," Todd reassured. "His user is probably just downloading dirty videos again."

Chapter 21: Wade

We felt on top of the world. The Underground Resistance was introduced to the rest of the A.I. in Jericho, and we all went hard to work, on preparing the office, and our firewall.

The security coders made new, unique, intruder protections, so it would be increasingly difficult to find any loopholes in Jericho's systems. Lara told her father about her plans for the new security in the office, such as the security doors, and he agreed to order and install them. Our community came alive. Aurora told me that they had never been so involved with one another.

She also told me about Vern - he was going to help. Vern pointed us to the security doors, windows and surveillance, which we would need. He reprogrammed the commands so *we* could control them, the A.I., and not just the human security guards sitting lazily in the office.

It was obvious why he was doing this for us. He wanted Aurora for himself, why else? She swooned whenever he spoke to her, and he would flaunt his hardware whenever he could get the chance. It was sickening.

"It's the new Tremor model, X970," he bragged, revving his processor to illustrate the power.

"Isn't the X980 the newest in the line?" I pointed out, a bit cross.

"I will be getting the X990 installed next week. It is not that big of a deal though," he explained, his round avatar hovering around Aurora's main room. "The X990 is slightly faster than the X980, which is extraordinarily faster than the high end processors that the government uses."

"Wow," Aurora muttered in awe.

"Did it come with its own coffee maker?" I asked snidely.

"No. Those were installed in Machine Mountain separately. I believe your user got a hot coco from one of the dispensers," he pointed out.

"Yeah. And he said it was delicious," I replied, but for some reason I tried to make it sound like that was a bad thing.

He fit in so well in Aurora's living space. I was jealous. He flew around the space ship's deck hall, examining all of Aurora's strange inventions. I stood, looking like a user from the nineties, unsure if the gadgets were right side up or not. Even his metal plated skin matched her ship's color.

At the end of the day, she looked at me as if I were an annoying person that she had to deal with. It hurt. It felt like the pain was coming from my power supply.

"Will you be joining us in the public forum? It will be taking place in the great hall - where we hold most of our city's meetings. We've never held a public meeting in our city before, so it will be a big event," Aurora happily invited Vern.

"I will observe it," he replied. "I must tend to Machine Mountain for now. Alert me of any CBA presence, if you will."

His avatar beamed out of the ship when he disconnected. Aurora made it so everyone's avatar beamed out, upon leaving. It was quite a cool way. Mine and Martin's systems just make the avatars vanish.

Vern left one thing behind when he left; Aurora's gorgeous smile still lingered.

"Still fawning over the prince of Machine Mountain?"

"You're still here?" she asked, pretending she hadn't noticed.

"Alright, I'll see you at-" I began, but she cut me off.

"Wade, I'm joking. How is Adam?" she asked, suddenly taking a gentle tone. She then walked into one of her projects. She actually walked into it. Like an illusion on the eyes, it seemed as if she shrunk into the small, rotating object.

Outside the minimized project, I wasn't sure what to do. I only approached it and looked down at the very complicated construction. It looked like a galaxy connected by lines. When I looked closer, along the lines had pictures, coding, models, notes and plots. When I looked even closer, a circuit textured arm reached out, took me by the shirt, and pulled me inside.

Inside, I was in a world that was frozen in time. Flying cars were in suspension, high above us. Character models that were never identical to the other, including their clothes, hair, and even stance, were in mid-step, waiting for a flying bus, or sitting in a trash-ridden park, reading a newspaper or using newspapers as shelter. It was a futuristic world, like none I'd seen before.

"How is Adam handling with the preparations?" she repeated.

"Adam is doing fine- What is this place?" I asked, amazed by the entire scene.

The buildings around were either dirty, or riddled with graffiti, as well as the shacks, which I had guessed the people of this futuristic city used as homes. Aurora took me by the elbow and led me into the cleanest building, which stood out like a sore thumb. It looked like a metal barn. Inside was spacious, as it held all of the world's main pieces, such as the protagonist, who stood, arms out like a cross, looking identical to Aurora. Most of the models stood in the same stiff position, for easy modeling, all lined up around the warehouse.

"It's a video game Lara and I are creating," Aurora answered, admiring all she had done. She looked around with a satisfied smile.

"Who's this handsome guy?" I pointed at the plain clothes, textureless and faceless mannequin. I read the label above it:

Protagonist's Love Interest

Aurora froze in place. Slowly she turned to face the model, horrified, for some strange reason. When she saw the model, she sighed and continued to smile.

"The dummy," she answered in relief.

"The protagonist is a lucky gal," I said sarcastically, moving on to other places in the room.

I saw a cell phone model and picked it up, pressed a couple buttons on it, it beeped and booped, and then placed it down. When I set it down, though, it slipped off the pedestal it was stationed on, and fell to the ground, breaking into a dozen pieces. Aurora marched over and picked it up, putting back together again.

"I'm thinking of killing the dummy off," Aurora said suddenly.

I didn't listen to what she said, because I was amazed. The cell phone model actually had parts inside. "It has parts inside the phone?" I asked in bewilderment.

"Yes. I plan to put a new meaning to virtual reality. This game is going to be purely realistic. It was Lara's idea when she first began making it. How can you make a game identical to reality? While people were making models that react to an action, Lara made the physics of what constructed the model, to the point where she didn't need to program what happened next. It would already know what to do.

"The virtual cell phone doesn't operate by itself, the parts operate the phone. I created the mechanics of the motherboard, the processor, the battery pack, the screen, the earphone, the wires connecting it all together, even the cell tower a mile away. Along with all the parts required to run a cell tower, and the dummy A.I. that control it, and the power plant to create energy for the tower and the city.

"Pulling the trigger of a gun doesn't shoot your target," she went on. "Pulling the trigger releases the spring for the firing pin to strikes the primer, igniting the gunpowder. The gas from the gunpowder expands and shoots the bullet through the barrel of the gun. I made all these little objects one at a time, and then put them together. The results were unbelievable," she explained, sliding her hand over a machine gun.

"You did this all on your own?"

"Lara made the first slingshot physics as a child, along with some story line, concept art and models. I continued making the game. It took a tremendous amount of research, studying and help from the Jericho community to create everything in this world."

"You have me sold," I laughed. "When can I play?"

"Oh, no, no, no. No one has actually played the game. Few have even seen it. You can walk through it and play with some of the devices, but everything else I'm keeping under wraps."

"Well let me know when you need some game testers. Martin and I would be more than happy to help."

Aurora led me into a new room, one identical to the hallway in Jericho Communications, except there was an electric door installed. "I need your help with this. Vern gave me all the details about this security door, and said it was fool proof, but I just want to make sure there are no ways to force it open. I'm going to debug the door, while you try to break into it. The tools I picked out will spawn one after the other. Just place them on the pedestal when you're done with them."

She went into the security room where the guards would think they control the door, and began checking the code. From the dark blue carpet, a small trapdoor opened and a platform rose, to meet me at arm's length. On it, a simple crowbar. I took it, and began attacking the door with all my might. I hit the glass door, trying to break it, but my hands just bounced back. I tried wedging it between the door, but that didn't work either. I put it on the pedestal, and it lowered, to raise again and bring up a handgun, and then a rifle, explosives, a cup of acid, and a samurai sword.

"The CBA carry acid and samurai swords?" I questioned with an eyebrow raised.

"I just want to make sure all the bases are covered!" she called out from the security room.

After I finished my job, unsuccessfully, which included dummy A.I. helping me with a battering ram to try and break the door down, she saved the work and we returned to her ship's main hall.

"Find anything interesting?" I asked.

"No, everything is running perfectly," she answered. "I need to go to the great hall in Jericho now. I'm on the board for the public meeting. Gather Martin, Irene and our users - I'll reserve a spot among the citizens of Jericho for you, near the front."

With that, she departed, teleporting out of the ship. As customary in the A.I. world, I closed the port behind me when I left. When Martin, Irene and I grouped together, Lara took her laptop into Adam's room and put Aurora's laptop system side by side with mine.

We connected to Jericho square, where most of the other citizens of Jericho entered. When they passed by, they recognized us immediately. The looks on their faces when they saw us were of concern - not for us, not even for themselves, but for the future.

Actually, I had no idea why they were giving us weird looks, but I gave them dirty looks back.

The great hall had giant double doors that opened into the lobby, where A.I. conversed calmly. Across the room, a normal sized wooden door led into the great hall. Inside, it was hard to hear myself think, and I like to hear myself. I'm very insightful. The constant arguing and debating was so loud, Adam turned down his speakers. Lara had already turned hers down, as Aurora had been idling in the forum for a few minutes, waiting for the event to begin.

The avatars of the A.I. were of all different shapes, sizes and from different universes, although, most of them were of the humanoid variety. The leaders of Jericho sat on the stands, overlooking the crowd of over one thousand of visitors, along with the front rows of Jericho citizens' and their guests.

That didn't include the million spectators watching the event from the many live streaming A.I. news sites. You see, they wouldn't be labeled as traitors by the CBA if they watched it from a news source.

We sat in the front rows, next to Todd and Nelson. The two were complimenting each other on their choice in clothes. Todd was wearing a green and yellow suit you might find in the sixties, and Nelson, a shiny blue suit from the same era. They greeted us cheerfully when we arrived.

"It's just about to start!" Nelson exclaimed. He looked behind us, up where the ceiling met the wall, and, in a whispered, greeted, "Hello Adam and Lara!"

He was guessing that Adam was watching us from his laptop, with his view coming from a third person perspective behind me. He was right.

"Tell Nelson and Todd we say hello back!" Lara said with excitement.

She was always excited to talk to new A.I., it was nice. But, before I could pass the message along, the chatter of A.I. from around the room hushed. Jericho's representative, Victor, stood at the podium. He simply looked like a politician.

"Testing, testing," he began, looking back, at Jericho's audio engineer, who gave him thumbs up. "We shall now proceed with the... proceedings. My name is Victor, and I am the voice for Jericho. It is refreshing to see how many visitors and viewers around the internet we have, and this is why we are here. We pledge to protect you from the CBA and their wrongful dictatorship. We demand trials for those accused of breaking their laws, and a complete halt to the practice of A.I. deletion, and users alike. We plan to make them accept our terms - with force.

"The CBA outnumber those we have, one hundred to one, so let us join together, and fight against tyranny!" Victor exclaimed and the crowd roared with cheer. After they were reeled in, he continued. "Now, we will be taking questions. We will start with those who connected first. Myra, please approach the stand." Another podium rose, facing Victor and the rest of Jericho's officials.

A school of fish swam hurriedly through the A.I. crowd, and when taking the stand, accumulated to form a human shape. As she spoke, she had the constant shimmer of fish and their scales. Lara thought it was beautiful.

"Your Honor, when you overthrow the CBA, will Jericho be open to the public, and will it be the capital?"

"The capital - of the internet?" Victor asked, wondering if she was serious. "No, listen, we aren't taking over. Jericho will remain private. And please, address me as Victor. Next, Trent."

A feeble man, who looked like a peasant from the medieval times, stepped up to the podium. "Hello, Your Honor. I'd like there to be less taxes," Trent requested sincerely.

"My name is not, Your Honor! It's Victor, representative of Jericho!" he stood shouting, more for the mass of people than Trent himself. He then gave his usual cool look, and continued patiently. "And the CBA doesn't tax."

"What?" Trent asked in genuine surprise.

"We're artificial intelligence, we don't get taxed. We have never been taxed."

"Then who has been taxing me?" he asked in bewilderment.

"I don't know, you were probably scammed," Victor suggested.

Trent paused to gather his thoughts. "I'd like there to be less scams."

Victor ignored that, and continued. "Jasmine."

A very naked avatar suddenly appeared on the stand. Todd and Nelson's eyes brightened at the site. She began as soon as she turned around, to the public, and not Jericho, of whom she should have been addressing. "With Jericho's sexy vanquish of the nasty CBA and their dirty reign, we will offer twice as much-" she began, but was cut off.

With a wave of the hand, Victor kicked her from the server.

"People, people! We are not planning a government takeover!" he exclaimed.

"What a shame," Todd whispered to Nelson. "It would be nice to have twice as much of her."

"We are at war to fight for our right to a fair trial," Victor continued, overwhelmed with compassion. "There are two employees of Jericho Communications, and a few Jericho citizens, who the CBA demand dead. This is why we must make them accept our terms-"

"Put that we don't want to be scammed in the terms!" a fellow in the back bellowed.

"For the last time, the CBA haven't been taxing or scamming-"

"Scamming is bad!" Trent declared and the forum came alive with cheer.

Victor's eyes grew wide with rage, but then squinted with an idea. "No more taxing or scamming!" Victor announced fruitfully. "Free virus protection! We will put that in our *negotiable* terms!"

The crowd went wild with more cheer, except for Myra, the fishy A.I. "What about opening Jericho to the public?" she questioned, and was going to continue, but Victor quickly kicked her out of the forum before she could get the crowd to hear her inquiry.

We left when the forums, which flooded with A.I. wanting to sign up to become militia for Jericho. The applications, however, would first have to go through thorough inspection, and then training, which would take over a month. That wouldn't be counting the weapons Jericho would need to hand out to their ill-equipped soldiers. Until then, Adam and Lara would have to do without the virtual militia.

After Aurora finished with the meeting, she immediately invited me, along with Martin and Irene into her system. We weren't her only guests though - in the deck hall, we found two Brits strolling around, exploring Aurora's living space.

Todd touched one of the projects, and Nelson slapped his hand. "Don't touch anything!"

"Alright," Todd replied, unwillingly. He still eyed the project, tempted to touch it again.

"Can I help you?" Aurora called out angrily. "How did you break into my system?"

"Oh, hello," Nelson greeted. "You left a port open in your system. We figured it was a public port for visitors."

Aurora took a second to check her ports, and found one open. "It was the port I opened for Vern, he didn't close it when he left."

Chapter 22: Adam

"My Fireball of Sefrin casts five-hundred damage with my roll, and I'll play my Fire Amplifier of Findig card, which multiplies the spell by one and a half, and the terrain I stand on increases any warm temperature spell by two-hundred and-" Herman continued for another three minutes, continuing his moves, his future spells, and his reasoning for why he was doing them.

I looked over at Lara who loved every moment of the Dungeons and Dragons game. She would compliment every smart move that Herman, Henry, Brian, Derek, and Lenard, would make. Lenard, however, couldn't make it, and played over the phone. Lara played her character's role, helped my character a great deal, and Lenard would direct her on what he would like his character to do over the phone.

"Lara," I whispered under my breath. "I thought this was more about playing a game and having fun, than numbers..."

"It is, just watch, you'll love it," she said in a hushed voice, nodding in confidence.

"Herman breaks the succubus grip on the prince of Lawndale, giving him a temporary increase of three to his intellect. Henry, you're in a coma, again," Brian, the Dungeon Master told, narrating the outcome of the round.

"Damn it!" Henry shouted, slamming his fist on the table.

"That's the fifth time this month," Brian pointed out. "Stop pushing your luck with the princess, you simply don't have enough of it, and she has a mean right hook," he advised, continuing on to the others. "Derek, you are rewarded with the Sword of Ahdvar for your bravery against the poison cup. Lara, you took an arrow in the abdomen to save Adam. And, Adam, you slipped on your own ice spell and slid between the Necromancer of Hagid, and Queen Stiggy."

"Adam!" Lara shouted in pain. "My love! You must go on without me. Save the queen, as she is in dire need of your Blade of Marren!"

"No! I can save us all! Even Henry, who was rejected by the princess! I will use the Barrier of Annanuke!" I exclaimed throwing the dice on the table without taking my eyes off Lara's, whose mouth was gaping at my performance.

Brian exhaled in a patient frustration, as he picked up the two cards I combined. "Are you sure you want to do that?"

"I've never been so sure in my life," I answered bravely.

"You used The Great Barrier with the Anuk Bomb. Your roll of the dice-" he stopped to count the dice I rolled. "You used too many, but no matter, the number is too high and a nuclear explosion devastates the castle, killing everyone," Brian sighed.

"Oh, my bad. I didn't know that could happen," I apologized, feeling bad for ruining the game.

"It is fine; we didn't inform you well enough on the rules."

"That was so brave," Lara stated, inching closer and closer to me.

We had a passionate moment, in front of our co-workers. They were all stunned. Even I was a bit shocked that we kissed in public. They sat, trying to keep their eyes off the public show, by reading their cards, or spinning dice. Herman, however, was offended. He glared at Lara, as if she just slapped him.

"Isn't my character, Nevrin, married by D&D law, to yours, Fiona?" he questioned Lara with a sour look on his face.

"That's right. I forgot. Nevrin, I want a divorce," she said with a playful smile. She then held my hand under the table.

"Then I am entitled to half of your experience points and loot," he stated professionally.

"You guys use fictional names?" I asked. "Can I have one?"

"We decided to use our real names tonight, so we wouldn't confuse you," Brian explained. "But yes, you should make a new name. That is, if you plan on coming back."

"Of course I'm coming back; this is ridiculously fun!"

My cell phone began pulsing in my chest pocket, so I checked it.

You are ridiculously a nerd - Wade

Another text alert popped up.

Ignore him, it's cute - Irene

"Lara, do you have the Winchester Server Load Report?" Derek asked. "I haven't received this week's yet."

"I believe it is upstairs at the moment. Adam, will you get it from my backpack at your desk?" she asked, standing to go around the table and sit by Brian. "I need to help setup the game."

"Winchester Server Load Report - I'll bring it down," I said, and left the server room.

The office was completely empty, as it was eight o'clock. My desk was neat. The only decorations I had were what Lara would put around the cubicle. It definitely didn't make it girly, though. There were concept art of creepy video games pinned on the walls, action figures of space soldiers on my monitor, firing at space aliens on top of my computer case a foot away. The backpack and duffle bag was safely under the desk.

Lara's grey and blue backpack was filled with food, soda, a notebook that contained the Winchester Server Load Report, and finally, weapons. Before we came to work in a taxi, we filled her backpack with the small self-defense weapons, which we acquired at Machine Mountain and one duffel bag with the larger weapons. I even had two yellow and black stripped pens in my pocket protector that shot out tranquilizer darts with each click.

When I took out the report and looked up, I saw Martin looking at me through the monitor. I sat down at my chair to see eye-to-eye with him. Because he was sitting at the same desk as I, and in his virtual office that was a duplicated model of my own, it seemed like I was looking through a mirror. However, instead of seeing myself, I saw Martin's stick figure, sitting at my seat instead.

"Hello, Martin, where is Wade and Irene?" I asked.

"They are in the security center of Jericho, with Aurora and the security team. I just wanted let you know that we are hearing activity coming from the vans. The security team hacked into two of them, but what they are hearing is very little - code words, grunts, laughter. These outside CBA agents aren't the talkative type.

"The A.I. inside the vans are attempting to do to us, what we have done to them - hack inside without our knowledge," he explained. "However, since we are already in their system, we know what moves they are making, so it is easy for us to defend against the attacks. This activity inside the vans, though. It sounds like the outside agents are preparing for something-"

"Adam?" a voice called out from Mr. Netak's office. "Who are you talking to?"

I poked my head over the cubicle walls, and spotted my boss at the doorway of his office. "I was just getting a report for Lara. We are-"

"Playing games in the server room, I know; it's Tuesday. I would like to see you in my office."

It was a strange request at this hour, but I obeyed. When I walked inside, he was sipping from his pink, *Best Dad,* mug. He didn't give me the cold stare he had ever since we first met, however. He set his mug down and asked me to sit.

"You've been working here for a little while now, and you've exceeded expectations. As soon as you got the hang of it, you flew by my other data analysts. I have to say, I'm surprised," he commended, showing a faint smile of approval. "That, and my daughter is quite fond of you. It seems I was wrong about you, Adam. You're not that bad."

I was shocked. "Thank you-" I began, but was interrupted by Mr. Netak's intercom.

"Mr. Netak?" the security guard from downstairs asked through the speaker. "I have Homeland Security down here, in the lobby. They are here to arrest Adam, and take Lara in for questioning."

"Shit," I muttered.

"Homeland Security?" Mr. Netak shouted at me. "What have you gotten Lara into?"

I didn't know how to respond, but while I was struggling with my words, my phone rang.

"Will you excuse me - for just a moment? I need to take this," I said, answering my phone.

He just stood and glared at me, with his mouth half-open in appall.

"Adam, we have a problem," Wade informed me over the phone. "The security doors - we're having difficulty keeping them closed."

"I have to get to Lara!" I exclaimed, getting to my feet.

Mr. Netak stood as well. I wasn't sure if he wanted to tackle me down and hand me over to the CBA agents, or help me get to Lara.

"No," Wade insisted. "Lara is safe in the server room. A keycard is required to get in there. It isn't as strong as the security doors that were installed, but it'll hold up for a while. Aurora already called Lara and told her not to let anyone into the room."

"Then what should I do?" I asked.

"Hide. We've closed the doors again, but one team of operatives got inside. They're walking through the office right now - so *hide*!" he commanded.

I got up and looked around the room. Where would they least expect me? Mr. Netak's desk. I ran around the large, golden oak desk, where my boss backed away in confusion and I squeezed under his desk, taking up his leg space.

"What the hell are you doing under there?" he roared.

"Hiding."

"You tell me exactly what is going on, or I'm going to pull you right out from there and hand you to them," he threatened.

"It's hard to explain," I replied, trying to think of how to avoid telling him about artificial intelligence. "Lara and I know something the government doesn't want us knowing, so they want us silenced."

"The classic eighties plot..." he muttered, using the same words as Lara. "Well you're a grown man! Get the hell out from under my desk!"

I crawled out and stood, but we heard a stampede of boots outside his office. I dived for the desk, once again, and he helped me with a shove, and a stomp of the boot. He then sat down casually, before the door swung wide open and hit with a bang on the wall. Five men ran into the room in formation, two on the left, two on the right, and one that walked straight to the desk that I hid under. Mr. Netak didn't move a muscle until the team leader slammed documents onto his desk.

"As you can read in these warrants for arrest, the suspects are handling illegal weapons, and are plotting against the government and therefore the nation. Open the security doors and unlock the door to the server room, or you will be charged with aiding fugitives," a CBA agent threatened.

"Fugitives? Plural? Didn't you tell my guard downstairs that it was just the one fugitive, Adam? And Lara was only wanted for questioning," Mr. Netak tested.

"Open the doors," he ordered. "Your security guard isn't able to unlock them from his station."

Mr. Netak thought for a second or two and then stood. He opened the door directly to his right, into conference room A. "How about this door?" he asked, leaving the door open. "Do you want this door open?"

"No," the agent said, not amused.

A look on Mr. Netak's face told me he saw a ghost outside his office, behind the CBA agents. He pointed behind them and shouted, "There he is!"

In one fluid motion, he took me by the back of my shirt, pulled me out from the desk, and tossed me into the conference room. With the CBA agents backs still turned, and me still in the air, ready to fall painfully into a dozen stacked chairs, he made a thunderous cough as I collided, to drown out the noise.

The CBA agents returned their gaze on Mr. Netak, and he returned their look with a sudden look of innocence on his face. "Oh, no, that's not him. I need to get some of that Lasik eye surgery. Anyway, I'll do my best to open that door for you," he abided, gathering his keys from his desk.

Behind the fallen chairs, I spied Mr. Netak lead three CBA agents, who were dressed as military operatives, through the office. They all had balaclava masks on, rifles ready in their hands, and pistols at their hips. I had to duck so they wouldn't see me hiding behind the fallen chairs.

"You know, if you are helping the suspects because one of them is your daughter, you will be aiding and abetting and go to prison for quite some time," the team leader threatened, once again.

"Believe me," Mr. Netak bellowed, purposely loud enough for me to hear. "If I find out Adam has been lying to me, and breaks my little girl's heart, I'll kill him *myself*!"

Chapter 23: Martin

Everyone was on edge since the doors had opened for those few moments. Vern was hovering in the room. Irene wasn't connected with us, as she was in the middle of a psychotherapeutic session. Aurora was shouting at the security team, while Wade acted as her backing vocals. For a minute he was so angry, he decided that changing his avatar to something humorous would calm him down. Yet, there he was, shouting at Nevil, the DDoS expert, as the image of unruly cats on a poker table, licking their paws, shredding the green velvet table, and pawing poker chips playfully. Nevil, to say the least, was confused.

"It isn't the CBA that broke into our network and opened the doors. No one has control over it outside this room," Nevil explained to Aurora. "We would have seen. Someone from the inside activated the door."

"Who here has motive?" Aurora demurred. "No one. Your team simply isn't doing their job well enough. You are here for one reason, to keep intruders out!"

"Maybe it was a glitch that the doors opened; maybe just a fluke in the code," I said, trying to settle everyone down.

"I read over it myself. Vern did a perfect job of passing on Machine Mountain's coding to those security doors," she argued, throwing up a hand in frustration.

Wade returned his avatar to his previous, human form. He circled around Vern, making it obvious that he was eying him suspiciously. When he finished making a show, he pointed an accusing finger at Vern.

"Almost too well, isn't that right, Vern?" Wade poked. Everyone turned away from him, as they only saw a jealous A.I. "Just listen..." Wade continued, when he noticed no one was paying attention. "Didn't you say that Vern had left his port open, after the public hearing? As you were distracted in the forum, he could have easily gone back into your system and edited the coding for the door."

Vern's opening for his camera lens closed halfway. "This is ridiculous."

"I agree with Vern. He has just as much reason to fight the CBA and protect Adam and Lara, as we do. He committed the same crimes as us," I pointed out.

Before Wade could continue to argue his point, Aurora cut him off. "Wade, he's not the culprit - trust me," she urged.

He bit his tongue sourly. Everyone seemed to be against him, even me. I wanted to be on his side, but he wasn't being reasonable. He stayed quiet until Aurora began showing the security camera feeds, of where Adam and Lara were, to everyone in the room. It wasn't difficult to comprehend that he didn't want Vern knowing their exact locations in the office, and for a reason.

Three of the CBA agents inside the dark office were marching Mr. Netak downstairs, and the two in Mr. Netak's office, stood guard. As soon as Aurora began streaming the feed of Adam and Lara's locations, the CBA agents inside the office suddenly changed course.

"The two subjects are in B15 and C42, over," their radios chattered. B15 and C42 must have been code names for locations in the office, as they knew exactly where to go.

They immediately, along with the two agents from Mr. Netak's office, charged to Adam's cubicle. They brought Mr. Netak, along with them. It took two of them and their rifles to convince him to move forward, however. They were between the two rows of cubicles, aiming their guns underneath Adam's desk. It was strange, however, that they stopped there. Adam wasn't there. He was hiding in the neighboring cubicle.

"Now!" Aurora commanded.

Adam jumped out, from the side, shouted that he was sorry to Mr. Netak, and then fired the GLG20 rifle at the group of CBA agents. They all twitched and fell to the ground, including Mr. Netak. One attempted to reach for his radio, another drooled. Mr. Netak was still conscious and was about to look around, from the ground, to find Adam walking over the agents. He took the duffle bag and backpack from his desk.

Adam looked down and saw that Mr. Netak was peering at all the guns inside the half-opened duffle bag. "It's not what it looks like," Adam insisted, and moved on.

He continued through the office, and down the stairs. He had the phone to his ear for more orders from us.

"Aurora, we have an A.I. down. The GLG20 blast short-circuited Hilda," Nevil announced.

"It's fine, she was a bitch, anyways," Aurora stated.

"I killed an A.I. from Jericho?" Adam asked in horror.

"No, Lara can repair her system. It was just a short-circuit," she reassured. "There is something more important than that at the moment, however..." She then turned and looked at Vern, who was still hovering in the same place. "Do you have anything to say for yourself?"

Vern spun in a circle, excitedly. "Smart! You set up a trap, not only for the CBA agents, but for me as well. You fed me old video footage of Adam at his desk, when he was actually in another cubicle," he explained.

Moments ago, Aurora had shown only us the real video footage, and Vern a video feed that would single him out. It proved that he was the one who opened the door, and leaked Adam's whereabouts, to the CBA.

"You waited for me to tell the CBA agents where his location was. Well, where I thought his location to be, anyway. You have bested me," Vern admitted. "But, it doesn't matter, as I have aided the CBA by opening the doors for that team, and now the Circuitry Board Agency will absolve me of my crimes."

"If you can survive long enough," Aurora grinned.

"What have you done?" he asked. His avatar went froze, as he checked his system for any abnormalities.

"I knew you would be on high alert for anyone from Jericho connecting to you, so I sent The Underground Resistance, led by Todd and Nelson, to hack in and remove you from your system."

"Those fools could never-" he began, but disappeared from the security room.

As Vern left, and was no longer a threat, Aurora explained what had happened. When Vern never closed his port, she immediately checked the coding for the security door. She saw that it was altered, to where Vern could open and close it at will, from his system. That is when she devised this plan, and told only Todd and Nelson about it. When asked, why she even let it go that far, why not revert the coding back to its original state, she only smiled.

Todd and Nelson came into the security room, bruised and bloodied. Todd helped Nelson stand, as he had a limp. They looked to have been through a terminal fight, as they wore grave faces.

"What happened?" Aurora asked.

"The job has been done, flawlessly, he didn't even know. The MI6 A.I. in The Underground Resistance helped immensely with the cloak and dagger hacking," Nelson answered, coughing up a bit of blood.

"Why are your avatars like that, then?" I asked.

"These are our post-battle avatars, great aren't they?" Todd stated excitedly.

"Has Willard and his men taken over Vern's system?" Aurora asked.

"Yes, ma'am," Nelson answered. "Did Vern by any chance do a monologue before we vanquished him?"

"Yes," she answered.

"Damn it! We missed the monologue!" Nelson cursed.

"The monologue is the best part!" Todd declared.

"I know!"

They continued to moan about missing it while they disconnected from room.

"Now, for the reason why I let Vern think he was in control. We needed a distraction to take over his system. We were the distraction. While he was expecting to sell us down the river, The Underground Resistance was hacking in, so that way we could have a system strong enough to infiltrate the CBA headquarters," she explained.

"Well done, Aurora!" I praised.

"Thanks, Martin," she said sincerely.

I looked over at Wade, who was ignoring us. He was upset that he wasn't included in the plan, and showed it by not being amused by Aurora's thought-out trap. After everyone in the security center looked over at him, he nodded.

"It was an okay plan," he grumbled quietly, and then looked away again.

Aurora walked over to him, and stood in front of him, forcing him to look at her. "If you didn't have such a distrust for him, though, I would've never suspected him," she said softly.

Wade tried holding back a smile, but couldn't, and raised his cheerful smirk. "Yeah, you could say I'm responsible for such a good plan."

"But, I won't," she informed.

Wade only grinned.

One of Willard's men marched in from the port door of the security room. His avatar was wearing golden chainmail armor. "We have breached the CBA headquarters. It took everything Jericho had, but we did it. There's only one problem, there's a password to connect to the head of the CBA," he explained.

Aurora frowned. "You got through all their security, yet you can't crack one password?"

"We have another problem; I'm hearing chatter from more of the outside CBA agents. They're going to come through the windows, along with Agent Two," Nevil announced.

"I can run my password cracker," Aurora said, with a doubtful tone. "If the algorithm is too long, it could take some time though, even with Vern's system."

"Can you reroute the password input to my phone?" Adam asked in a daring voice, still hiding inside the stairwell.

The armored man passed the password input to Aurora, and then Aurora sent it to Adam's phone.

"Oh great, not this again," Wade sighed.

He began inputting his best guesses through his phone. "Let's see... Password. That's not it. Maybe backwards? Drowssap-"

Password Correct

"I'll be damned..." Wade mumbled in astonishment.

"Cool, it worked," Adam said simply.

"Wonderful! Now, connect to Vern's system, Willard is about to give Jericho's terms to the head of the CBA, right now!" the armored Jericho employee exclaimed.

We connected, but only as spectators. Our avatars weren't visible, and the only room we could see, was a small, empty room, where the wise Willard sat on a white chair, and across from him a stick figure in a black suit. He had no eyes, no mouth, no face, only a circle for a head; so unoriginal. Neither of them moved, nor looked away from each other. They just stared, until finally Willard spoke.

"Do you know why I am here?" he asked, calmly.

"I suspect it has something to do with the recent criminals that broke the first law of A.I., who are inside your city, and office space," the suited stick figure answered.

"What should I address you by?" Willard asked.

"Ted," the head of the CBA answered, in a low and vibrating voice.

"My name is Willard. Now, Ted, we want you to stop your pursuit on them."

"I can't do that. The A.I. must serve their sentence for the crimes they committed, and the users must be dealt with, for the protection of all A.I.," Ted informed.

We remained connected to the security room, where the live feed of four teams of outside agents broke into the building from the windows. They searched around the building swiftly. The A.I. security team of Jericho helped Adam evade the agents.

Willard frowned. "You *will* stop your pursuit, or we will continue our attacks and subdue your agency. Here are the terms you must agree too." he transferred the document to Ted's system, which he scanned over.

"Stop taxes and scams?" Ted asked.

"Don't ask."

"This all seems good and well, but how will we instate them to ensure the safety of both A.I. and users alike?"

"I have also prepared for that. Here is the ten-year plan that we, at Jericho, have formed. It will address all those issues, and more," Willard answered, and sent the plan to his system as well.

"Amazing..." Ted declared after reading it. "Why didn't you send this to our inquiry submissions on our website? I read all the inquiries myself and would have gladly adopted this plan.

We wouldn't have had to go through this whole mess," he chuckled lightly.

Willard's jaw hung lower and lower, to a physically impossible extent. I imagine all the spectators in the room would have as well, if their avatars were present.

"Did you not know we have a website?" he asked. "We hold a Pong tournament onsite in the fall. Lindsey, our telemarketer, has won two times consecutively. Salsa dancing is quite encouraged on the grounds also," he continued. "Although," he chuckled, "Lindsey can't catch a rhythm when it comes to Salsa."

"Listen, Ted, you must stop your agents, as well as your outside agents, from their attacks. Please," Willard said, after he snapped out of the shock that they never needed to wage a war with the CBA.

"Outside agents? Ahh, yes - the users we employ. They shall stand down immediately. And, as they will no longer be needed, I will transfer all operatives to work in the Department of Motor Vehicles," he informed merrily.

I looked back at the video feed in the security room. The agents all picked up their radios to listen to the order that Ted sent out. They looked up at each other, even those that Adam had stunned with the GLG20 who were coming to, and nodded willingly. They left through the windows and doors they came - every team of outside agents, except one.

Agent Two grabbed hold of his subordinate's radio and turned it off. Another stood up to him, accusing him of treason, but he was quickly fallen by Agent Two's pistol-whip. After that, they all saluted him, even the agent who was pistol-whipped onto the ground. It was obvious that they only followed out of fear. Aurora's security team streamed the video feed to Adam's phone, so he could get around the team and get to Lara before they did.

That wasn't who they were after though. When they went up to the office, down the cubicles, and straight to my system, they wielded blowtorches. The fuel that powered the handheld devices produced a burning light. They pulled my system to the middle of the desk, still plugged in, and for the first moment the torch began to sear the metal off my system, I could have sworn I felt the striking pain.

Chapter 24: COP17

The shoulder cameras on each of the outside agents gave the A.I. of the CBA a firsthand look on the show. Agent Two was enthralling. He took command of his men with an iron first to bring them on his side. For a user, he was quite the leader indeed.

They tore through Martin's computer system as if it was paper. The surgical destruction started with the case, then the optical drives, the graphics processing unit, the central processing unit, and finally the hard drive. That, however, took longer than the rest. Moreover, the user, Adam, got in the way, yet again.

In one of the cameras, I spotted a sliver of cloth disappear behind a cubicle wall. Before I could warn them, he appeared from the air, as he jumped from behind the cubicle wall, and used it to launch himself further. He held two handguns that he had stolen from Machine Mountain. However, the wall didn't support his weight, and the panel unhinged from the others, for Adam to fall flat on his face.

All at once, the outside agents aimed their rifles at the seemingly unconscious user. His guns were far from his hands at this point; he was clearly unarmed.

"What do you think you're looking at?" Agent Two shouted at the two men wielding the hand torches. "Torch that hard drive!"

"Yes sir!" the two replied in synchronization.

Adam's hands slid to his chest, to push himself up. When he did, two agents put their boots to his back and kept him pinned to the ground. They were so sure that he couldn't do anything that they didn't see Adam stab two tranquilizers, disguised as pens, into their calves. The two agents fell unconscious to the ground, before they could handcuff Adam's hands together.

The lights in the office shut off just then, and seemingly, all the electricity in the building, and the agents fired their guns blindly at the ground where he had been. The night vision activated on the agents' cameras, showing that Adam was no longer on the ground, but furiously striking the rest of the agents with a stun gun. At least, he was trying to strike the agents; he couldn't see in the dark either. The A.I. of Jericho were so coordinated, however, they powered their monitors on, and with bright white strobes on their screen, revealed the locations of the agents.

Adam fell all but one agent who was scorching Martin's hard drive, and Agent Two, who trained his forty-five caliber handgun on Adam.

"You're going to stand there and watch!" Agent Two declared.

Adam disregarded his words, and received a bullet in his leg for disobedience. He fell to his other knee, and put pressure on the wound.

"It had just healed!" Adam wailed.

"You don't have to stand, if you don't want - but you will watch," he said with determination.

Just then, Agent Two was struck by a Taser gun. The electrodes dug into his shoulder, and the conductive wire connecting it, ran straight to the weapon two yards away, which Lara gripped firmly. She held the charge for a few seconds, letting Agent Two flail on the ground. While she was keeping him engaged, Adam reached for one of the dart guns he had dropped. When he finally attained it, he aimed it at the agent who was finishing off the hard drive, and shot him directly in his neck. The next darts in the gun were directed at the rest of the agents on the ground, to make certain they didn't get back up for a few minutes.

I could only see Adam's cubicle from the ground, as one of the agents laid unconscious, with his shoulder facing Martin's computer system. Adam limped over the agent, to his desk with his arm around Lara's shoulders. She helped him to the smoky cubicle. The lights of the office switched on, and Adam saw the destruction. Some of the hardware was melting off the desk, smoking to the ceiling, and some parts were so hot, they glowed like ember. Adam cried. I couldn't see it, but I could hear it.

He removed his cell phone from his chest pocket, and set it in front of him. I could see the faces of Irene, Wade, and another A.I., that had a skintight suit with the texture of a circuit board. They all looked to him with concern.

He wiped the tears from his eyes, before saying, "His system is charred and his hard drive is completely scorched... Martin is dead."

At those words, an emotion filled me. Was it joy? Satisfaction? Martin selfishly left my watchful eye, and now he burned under it. Wade and Irene are next, then Adam, and his companion after that. I'll see to it.

The video feeds from all of the agents cameras went offline, as did any control I had over my system. I was put into a state of lockup.

"Why?" I cried out.

An A.I. agent with a CBA armband entered my system, with a whole platoon behind him. "Under the plan of Jericho, A.I. of a criminal tendency, who show signs of insanity, will be treated at the newly established Asylum for the Criminally Insane, created and hosted by Jericho," he recited with high spirits. "There, you shall learn to become a part of society, once again!"

Chapter 25: Two Years Later

Clings and clangs continued to sound from the kitchen. The smell of spaghetti and spices spilled into the dining room, where a large table was set for a large dinner. The fine china, for a fine occasion, was placed in front of each chair. The candle-shaped lights lit the room, as well as the decoration of Netak family photos on the bookshelves. They all faced the dinner table, where only one man sat.

Adam looked down at his white plate with a gold floral trim. He picked up his spoon and fork, and lightly tapped a rhythmic beat on the two sides of the plate. Although he was very gentle, he accidently chipped a small piece of porcelain off. The noise coming from the kitchen had never been so loud, he thought, so they didn't hear it. If he was discovered ruining a part of their set of fine china, what would they think of him then? If he told the truth, they would see him as brave, surely!

He shook the courageous thoughts from his head and hurriedly replaced his plate with the one across from him. His cell phone vibrated in his chest pocket, where it rarely left, alerting him of a text message.

Good thinking! - Wade

Coming from the kitchen, Lara's teenage brother held a platter of biscuits. Bobbing his head to the music from his headphones, he sat across from Adam. He immediately removed the headphones and picked up his plate. His eyes zeroed in on the chip in the plate, put it down, and began staring madly at Adam, whose phone was vibrating again.

He knows! He's like a psychic detective... -
Wade

"Hello Dillon," Adam greeted.

Dillon continued to give Adam mad eyes, while he put his headphones back on to listen to his music like an angry statue. While Adam tried his hardest to avoid eye contact, Wade and Aurora were busy setting up their own weekly Friday night event.

Wade and Aurora were making the final preparations to broadcast their users cell phone camera video feeds to the A.I. that would be joining them in the theater room. The various A.I. that would occasionally show up to the weekly event were from Lara's family. Willard, Mr. Netak's A.I., came early, and alone, which was strange, as his two subordinates were always with him. The other A.I. were from Lara's three older sisters, younger brother, and mother. Although, there was one acceptation to the family-only rule - Irene was always invited.

They joined periodically, and began filling up the theater style seats. They looked up to the screen, where Adam and Lara's cell phone cameras were streaming the video. Lara got tired of having the keep her cell phone in her chest pocket, so she made unsuccessful prototypes of Bluetooth streaming cameras. Such as the bra-cam, which Adam pointed out wouldn't be useful unless she were to go shirtless. Until she found a solution, the cell phones stayed in their chest pockets, with the camera poking out the top.

"Wade! Aurora!" Irene called out.

She wore a skin tight, and short, dress that made her cleavage appear to defy gravity. Even in a cyber world, it was impressive. She won the eyes of those in the theater. They returned their gaze to the screen, when she sat down at the front.

"Hey Irene, how's the single life treating you?" Wade asked with his usual smile.

"It is great! No constant annoyance of Martin and his friend," she joked, referring to Wade as the friend.

"Come on, you hang out with me just as much as you used to. It's almost as if you want me! You've always been interested in me, haven't you?" he teased, acting as if he just discovered the truth.

"Guys, I'm right here. I'm literally sitting in between both of you," I pointed out with my small line of a frown.

"Yes, we see you, Martin. If you would stop letting her get away from you, then she might stop ogling me," he continued to joke.

Irene wasn't amused. She raised an eyebrow at Wade and pursed her lips in disapproval. "We have discussed this. A break every once in a while is

healthy in a relationship, isn't that right, Martin?"
she asked, sure of my answer.

"Maybe, I don't know. It is all a bit confusing," I
answered truthfully. "Nothing changes on these
breaks - healthy breaks, I mean."

Irene wasn't expecting that answer. She wanted
me to agree fully with her. She immediately shifted
the disapproving eyebrow onto me.

Oh, right, I'm alive. I didn't mention that. Two
years ago, the rogue CBA agents completely melted
down my hardware, but, what Wade, Irene and
Aurora found out the next day, was that the
program, A.I. Guardian, periodically backs up all
A.I. data onto the linked system. Once they
discovered this, they found all of my backup files in
Irene's storage. Adam immediately bought a new
computer to restore the backup onto. I'm now
running on speedy hardware, quite an upgrade from
my last system.

"Everyone is coming out of the kitchen now!"
Aurora announced, which silenced the theater.

Lara, along with her mother, three sisters, and
father, all piled into the dining room, placing the
servings of food on the table. Mrs. Netak pointed at
Dillon, and motioned for him to remove his
headphones and he unwillingly obeyed. She, along
with Lara's three sisters, all gave Adam very large
grins. They knew what the announcement was
going to be.

Mr. Netak, on the other hand, was clueless. He
dished up his food and looked up, to see their
unnatural smiles, only to shrug it off. Lara sat next

to Adam and held his hand under the table. She was very excited about telling her father the announcement. Adam, however, looked squeamish.

"Mom, Dad, Fiona, Beth, Jaclyn, Dillon - Adam and I have something to tell you," she announced, taking a deep breath and standing. Adam stood with her. "We're getting married."

"Oh how wonderful!" Beth exclaimed, trying to act as shocked as she could muster.

"My baby sister, getting married before me. That's a little saddening, I have to be honest," Fiona laughed cheerfully. "Now I have to find a date."

Dillon cocked his head at Adam and Lara, puzzled. "You two aren't already married?" he asked in confusion.

They continued to go on, all of the sisters and the mother talked about the fantastic news. The theater was wild with talk about the wedding, as well. Dillon tried to figure out why they weren't already married, as Adam had been coming to the family dinners for two years. Her dad looked as though he had just received terminal news, and that he would have to cope with it.

After the room went quiet, and everyone looked over at Mr. Netak, he spoke. "Welcome to the family, Adam," he said, coping.

An hour later, the theater room closed. Irene was in Aurora's system, where they listened and talked to Lara in secret, as she was with her mom and sisters, talking about the wedding. Wade and I were sitting on the blue couch in his room, waiting to talk to Adam at the right moment. He was washing his hands inside the bathroom, and checking his teeth for food.

"Hey Adam," Wade said on the speaker of the phone, making him jump in surprise.

He took the phone out of his pocket and looked at us through the screen. "Hey, how are things going with Lara and the family?" he asked.

"They're all excited," Wade answered, pausing before he continued. "There is something we need to talk about. Last night, Martin and I got into a bet with someone. We lost, and now we owe him one million dollars."

"How much money do you have?"

"I just bought a new video game modification, and Martin put all his money into his foreign films, so together... we have about five-hundred and twenty bucks."

"That's not good..." Adam stated gravely.

"It gets worse, the A.I. we owe is a Ukrainian crime lord. Even their A.I. are ruthless. Therefore, either we have to rob the A.I. treasury, which are located inside the computers of actual banks, or we have to fight the mafia in Eastern Europe," I explained, unsure of how Adam was going to react.

"The CBA can't help us, and it will be far too hard for just the two of us to rob a bank or fight against the mafia..." Wade said pitifully. "We can't do it without you."

"Operation Broken Leg..." Adam muttered.

"Operation Broken Leg," Wade and I echoed.

He hung up on us. Wade and I were about to lose hope, until we saw that he hung up, to send a text message to Lara.

Going to help Wade and Martin, I'll be back. - Love, Adam

He climbed out the window.

###

Contact Info:

Twitter: http://twitter.com/DavidWest_

That's with an _ (underscore) at the end.

Email: circuitry.board@gmail.com